THE
LITTLE
BOOK
OF
HEREFORDSHIRE

THE
LITTLE
BOOK
OF
HEREFORDSHIRE

DAVID J. VAUGHAN

To Sarah

First published 2016

The History Press
The Mill, Brimscombe Port
Stroud, Gloucestershire, GL5 2QG
www.thehistorypress.co.uk

British Library Cataloguing in Publication Data.
A catalogue record for this book is available from the British Library.

ISBN 978 0 7509 6628 3

Typesetting and origination by The History Press
Printed and bound in Great Britain by TJ International Ltd

CONTENTS

ACKNOWLEDGEMENTS

There are many people to thank for their invaluable assistance in compiling this book. Melissa Seddon and her colleagues at Herefordshire Council (Historic Environment Record), for setting me straight on their heritage jewels; Tamsin Westhorpe and Joyce Marston of Stockton Bury Gardens, for their endless supply of historical nuggets; Melanie and Ray at Hereford Cathedral, for their generosity of spirit and abundance of time; Heather Hurley, for her sage advice during our all too-brief encounter; Matilda Richards at The History Press, for her editorial guidance; and to past experts and authors (dead and alive), whose own achievements have informed and inspired this new, modest effort.

Last, but *not* least, my wife Claire Vaughan, professional illustrator and artist. Her incredible drawings have raised this book to another level entirely. Claire, as in so many things, this would not have happened without you. All images (excepting those on pages 67, 82, 84, 104, 106, 146, 150, 169 and 180) are © Claire Vaughan.

Other Image Credits:

Grateful thanks to the following for their kind permission to reproduce images on the pages below:
British Library (p. 150) – © The British Library Board, K.top Vol. 15, 96.h.
Herefordshire Archive Service (p. 106) – BS67/4/2
Library of Congress (pp. 146, 180)

Finally, I have endeavoured (but failed) to include only places that are open to the public. Please always check arrangements (if any) and respect the privacy of present occupiers and owners. All information given has been to the best of my knowledge accurate at the time of writing. I apologise for any errors, oversights or omissions I may have unwittingly made. Nonetheless, I hope you enjoy the fruits of my labour.

David J. Vaughan, 2016

INTRODUCTION

When The History Press asked me to write *The Little Book of Herefordshire*, I was both daunted and proud. On the one hand, my family connections stretch back for more than two centuries, putting me in a good position to gather anecdotes and treasures from this county we love; on the other, I knew there were others more qualified to give the shire its due.

'Mr Hereford' himself, Richard Johnson, faced a similar challenge in 1868. In his own preface to *The Ancient Customs of the City of Hereford*, he summed up his – and my – heartfelt lament:

> The writer is aware that criticism may discover many defects in the present work, and that abler pens might hereafter do greater justice to the subject. He therefore requests his readers kindly to concede their indulgence for any imperfections, and only regrets that want of leisure for the thorough prosecution of his researches has rendered it necessary to omit many points of interest.

The infinite things worthy of mention are a source of worry: facts, achievements, successes and failures – all that have made Herefordshire great. As well as these there are the many examples left out: victims of limited space.

Even the most casual reader of the following chapters will glean quite how much the county has meant to the world down the ages …

In 'It's All a Matter of Time', people from before the eons of writing were already making their mark. From cave dwellings to stone tombs, hillforts to bronze work, prehistory laid down the foundations. Our ancestors since then have bequeathed a rich 'Heritage' collection – so vast, it demands more than the two chapters it shares.

Even as time passed, so too did its changing 'Environment'. Land, weather and climate brought both hope and despair: from infertile wasteland to life-giving crops, from the most prosperous sheep to its world-famous bull!

All the while Herefordshire has been a county worth having: a bold claim the truth of which is revealed in no greater way than in its 'Borderlands' fights. Hence, the county has the nation's greatest assemblage of castles and mottes.

Herefordshire has been shaped by its 'People'. Achieving fortune and fame, there have been stars who have gone on to shine long after their death. And there are those born outside its borders who have been drawn to a place worth making their own.

Sporting successes, present and past, have given rise to a rich world of 'Leisure'; closely matched by exponents from the world of the 'Muse' – art, architecture, theatre and music. All have brought intellectual riches and cultural charm.

Of course, for every success story there are one or two less favourable failures. 'Crime and Punishment' may have changed down the years, but the county's most successful attempts to be rid of bad behaviour came through its 'Education and Language' – whether English or Welsh, private or state.

But it is perhaps its deep-rooted 'Religion' and its ties with 'Royalty and Politics' that sets Herefordshire apart from the other counties of the United Kingdom. Kings have been made, usurpers despatched; religious houses established, political clout won and lost.

Through it all, there has been a singular constant: Herefordshire, this place we call home. A county unmatched.

1

IT'S ALL A
MATTER OF TIME

FROM ROAMIN' TO ROMAN

Period	Dates (c.)	Key Attributes
Upper Palaeolithic	100,000 BP* to 10,000 BCE*	Cave dwelling, hunting, exotic animals
Mesolithic	10,000 BP	Hunter-gatherers, the final thaw, early stages of settlement
Neolithic	4,000 to 2,800 BCE	Farming, long barrows, community
Bronze Age	2,800 to 700 BCE	Hierarchy, round barrows, metals, ritual
Iron Age	700 BCE to 43 ACE*	Hillforts, tribes

*BP = before present; BCE = Before Common Era; ACE = After Common Era

UPPER PALAEOLITHIC

Predating the written word, human history developed in the epoch of the Upper Palaeolithic, the final stages of the last Ice Age. In Herefordshire, due in part to its acidic soil, little evidence of our human ancestors has survived. That which has survived has astounded the greatest minds.

With *Homo sapiens* populating the Welsh Marches since before 50,000 BP, the county's human story is prodigious. At **Doward**, near Symonds Yat, two caves from the late Upper Palaeolithic – fancifully named Arthur and Merlin – conceded skeletal remains of woolly rhino, giant deer, hyena (!) and even mammoth. At least one human burial was also discovered, indicating ritual and an early compassion.

The majority of evidence from the period is concentrated at five local sites: Colwall, Kington, Sarnesfield and Tupsley, as well as Doward itself. The truth of Upper Palaeolithic life, though, was far more nomadic and, ultimately, you went where the food was abundant …

MESOLITHIC

The Mesolithic period saw a dissipation of the last tendrils of ice and a great migration of animals and hunters. Predator and prey moved into newly accessible areas with fresh vegetation. Midway through the epoch, it was still possible to walk a direct route from Denmark to France without wetting your feet!

The land now marked by the county boundary was colonised by some of the earliest trees and plants, as revealed by modern pollen accounts:

birch	alder	oak
willow	pine	hazel
aspen	lime	

The Golden Valley, Great Doward and the area around Ledbury have provided strong evidence for Mesolithic migration. Though as the area grew rich in natural resources, mobile hunter-gatherers gave way to a more settled way of life ...

NEOLITHIC

The Neolithic era was a period not only of sedentary farming but also of a rapid sense of community (egalitarianism). Collective ritual can be seen in the remains of the long barrows, erected as monuments to the ancestral dead, which contained not individuals, but a so-called 'body politic' – disarticulated long bones and skulls grouped separately within sealed, stone chambers (see Arthur's Stone, p.25). Other barrows were built on the site of mortuary houses, ritually burned and supplanted by stone (e.g. at **Dorstone Hill**).

By this point, Herefordshire was thickly wooded, but the long barrows and earliest stages of farming brought with them the clearance of vegetation, particularly in valleys or on top of the hills. Around **Buckton** (on Teme) and **Staunton-on-Arrow** are but two key examples.

With less time spent hunting, it was only a matter of time before the next technological breakthrough ...

BRONZE AGE

Bronze Age Herefordshire was, by now, devoid of much of its forests. So too, the community spirit, giving way to a more individual, hierarchical structure. The important and powerful (from war, metalworking, shamanism) were buried in *circular* barrows, as different to the collective long form as it was possible to get. And with it, great ritual: not just in funereal rites (which now included valuable grave goods) but in the construction of huge sacred centres: stone circles and henges, as suggested at **Marden** and **Clifford**. The living and dead monumentally scribed.

Towards the end of the era, great field divisions began to create a landscape, which we might recognise today. With these divisions came the segregation of the population into families, possibly even 'clans'. The last great deforestation not only produced settled existence but also what grew to become the centre of farming, the agricultural heartland we acknowledge today.

IRON AGE

The succeeding Iron Age brought a new world, a break with what came before: isolated communities and a great retreat into the enclaves of domestic and defensive abodes. Hillforts, like those at **Aconbury**, **Pyon Wood** and **British Camp**, all witnessed great violence: a mass burial in the ditch of **Sutton Walls** contained twenty-four skeletons. Between 5ft 8in to well over 6ft, these were men that had been strong in the body – and tooth, judging by the relatively few signs of decay.

ROMAN

When the Romans came, the largest (only?) Iron Age tribe in Herefordshire was either the *Dobunni* or *Silures*; though it might equally have been neither! Social and cultural evidence of both are still missing. More likely, then, it was the *Decangi* who Scapula, Roman governor of Britain, attacked before driving on into Wales.

Yet little has been found of Roman life in the county, and it is possible that the region remained a borderland launch – a place from which to conquer the Welsh. Over the border lay precious supplies, of gold, silver and lead.

Only at *Ariconium* (near Weston under Penyard) has extensive settlement been found (see p.33). Small forts, perhaps for supplying their army, existed at **Leintwardine**, while only small 'towns' have been found at **Blackwardine**, **Stonechester** and **Stretton Sugwas** (not far from Kenchester). Even the roads here were mere tributaries of their main northward thrust – the discovery of Watling Street at Leintwardine arguably the most daring exception.

SAXON

The Saxon age was the last great pre-modern era, whose people gave the county its name. The Mercian Saxons waged war for a land left behind by the Romans. Their great armies and *burhs* silenced the Welsh, while King Alfred himself made Hereford proud. But it was the Christianised clerics who arguably left more of a mark – men such as St Ethelbert the King (patron of Hereford Cathedral) and Earl Leofric, benefactor of Leominster.

SHIFTING SANDS OF GOVERNMENT

The history of Herefordshire government is more complex than most. With the fall of the Romans, the incoming Saxons at last took control. Swathes of land were absorbed in the province of Mercia – or, literally, 'land of the boundary dweller'.

Its relations with Wales and the Marches produced misusers of power. During violent engagements, large sweeps of the landscape oscillated between Welsh, English and Norman command. Particular tracts – *Arcenfelde* or Archenfield included (see p.17) – retained for a long time their own independence, kept apart from the laws of the land.

Herefordshire was not known by that name until the eleventh century, by which time Hereford proper had been a principal town for 300 years. The name (Here-ford) means 'ford of the army', most likely formed when the Mercian and *Magonsæte* dynasties fashioned a pact.

Since then, the county has been capriciously conflated and wrenched from the grasp of its (administrative) neighbours, Worcester, Gloucester and the old county of Shrews.

Athelstan, the first King of all Briton, established a Hereford mint, the first to appear along the course of the Severn.

Rare forays by Scandinavian Vikings occurred in the north of the county, as well as their sacking of Hereford *c.* 913. Twelve months later, along the Wye and the Severn, they ravaged Archenfield, before suffering defeat at the site known as Killdane Field (Weston-under-Penyard).

Twenty years after William I conquered Britain, by the time of Domesday (1086), Hereford was one of only sixteen great cities.

With the Conquest came a new breed of tyrant: the Marcher lords, whose Norman power controlled as much land as they grabbed. William's three newest earls – of Hereford, Shrewsbury and Chester – silenced the troublesome borders and took control of the March (land between England and Wales). They did so even in the face of new English resistance from the Mercian magnate, Eadric the Wild.

A SNAPSHOT OF HUNDREDS

The hundred in Herefordshire – a division of land recorded by William I equating to 100 households – is hideously snarled. No sooner had Domesday been written than the lands, and the hundreds, were radically changed. By the Middle Ages, they bore little resemblance to what had gone before.

Up to nineteen Herefordshire hundreds (with courts or *moots*) were listed in Domesday, though several were later 'migrated' into Gloucester and Wales, even Worcester across to the east. One, *Lenteurde* (Leintwardine), now firmly in Herefordshire, was then listed as Shropshire. The inconsistent spelling of place names was never that helpful, while the anomalies of *Arcenfelde* and *Stradel* only muddied the pitch!

Domesday Anomalies
Two anomalies, originally encountered in the Saxon–Welsh divisions, were inherited by Domesday. 'British' 'enclaves' or *commotes* (Welsh *cwmwd*) were recorded in the south and west of the county:

Archenfield (Arcenfelde) remained in practice, like its western 'cousin', *Ewias*, outside the hundred system of England. Its people were considered as Welsh, a claim underlined by the practice of paying rent in the form of *sestiers* of honey, as was that country's custom. The measure of land too was different, often recorded in *carucates* rather than the usual *hides*.

Punishment for misdemeanours also followed Welsh custom; such as that bestowed on a murderer, whose victim's 'kin were entitled to prey upon him and his kin, and to burn their houses, until the corpse was buried about noon of the following day' (Victoria County History 1908: 267).

Many believe the name *Arcenfelde* arose from Roman *Ariconium* (see above). Whatever the truth, it was eventually subsumed by the much later medieval hundred around Wormelow Tump.

Stradel – the River Dore, in the *valle Stradelie* (the Golden Valley), is thought to have been the boundary between the English and Welsh. Centred on the castle at Ewias (Ewyas) Harold (see p.57), the manorial seat was at Ewias Lacy (now Longtown). Remained outside the English hundreds until much later into the eleventh century.

HUNDREDS AT DOMESDAY

1 Bromesais/Bromesesce/Bremesse (Brooms Ash/Broxash)
2 Greitewes (Greytree)
3 Lene (in Eardisland)
4 Wimestruil/Wimstrui (Webtree)
5 Plegeliet
6 Urmelauia/Wermelau (Wormelow)
7 Elsedune
8 Dunre (Dinedor)
9 Tragetreu
10 Wimundestreu
11 Radelau/Radenelau (Radlow)
12 Hezetre
13 Cutethorn/Cutestorn (the area of Ewias, though it was not included)
14 Wlfagie/Ulfei (Wolfhay/Wolphy)
15 Stapel/Stepleset
16 Tornelaus/Tornlaws
17 Stratford/Stradford (Stretford)

18 Bradeford
19 Broadfield/Bradefelle
20 Arcenfelde/Arcenefelde (Archenfield)
21 Stradel/valle Stradelei (Golden Valley)

The following was then placed under Shropshire:

Lenteurde/Lenteurd (Leintwardine)

THE ANCIENT CUSTOMS OF HEREFORD

Through the Great Custom Book, or charter of King Henry II (1154–1189), the city of Hereford became the seat of medieval democracy. Its citizens, lords, clergy, even the monarch himself, were made to abide by mandated decrees. So successful was it that numerous towns, especially Ruthlan (*Drusslan*), and others in Wales, adopted its rules.

As well as democratically electing an annual bailiff, it delivered fair justice using the concept of jury, made up of no less than twelve good and true.

In 1189, after Henry had died, his son Richard I sold Hereford to its people – yet the Custom Book remained its principle guidance, and did so until Charles II was king.

HEREFORD MAYORS

An Act in the time of King Edward IV insisted that the Hereford mayor must remain in office no more than twelve months (seemingly to avoid nepotism and corruption). Such tricks to secure the privileges and emoluments of office had previously led to at least one suspiciously 'elected' twenty-one times! The rule was enforced 'upon pain of disenfranchisement' (made no longer a freeman in the said city of Hereford).

SHERIFFS OF HEREFORDSHIRE

The county's sheriff appears to have served as deputy to the earl, until the latter became more ceremonial and his once number two took over administering justice and managing the king's finances in this part of the world.

Here is a random selection of the holders of office since antiquity through to before George IV:

1086 (Domesday)	Bernai
r. Henry I	Hugoni de Boclande
r. Henry II	Walter de Hereford, William de Bello-campo
r. Richard I	William de Braose
r. Edward I	Milo Pychard
r. Henry IV	John ap Harry
r. Henry VIII	Thomas Baskerville
r. Elizabeth I	William Shelley
r. Charles I	Wallop Brabazon
Interregnum	Thomas Cook
r. Charles II	Robert Symonds (as in Symonds Yat?)
r. George III	(the delightfully named) Thomas Beebee

LORDS LIEUTENANT OF HEREFORDSHIRE

Traditionally a military role in the time of Henry VIII (r. 1509–47), the incumbent remains the monarch's representative in the county:

1690	Charles (Talbot), Earl (afterwards Duke) of Shrewsbury
1702	Charles, Duke of Shrewsbury, re-appointed on the accession of Queen Anne
1704	Henry (Grey), Earl (afterwards Duke) of Kent
1714	Henry, Duke of Kent, re-appointed on the accession of George I
1715	Thomas Lord Coningsby
1727	James (Brydges), Duke of Chandos
1741	Charles Hanbury Williams, Esq.
1747	John Lord Viscount Bateman
1760	Viscount Bateman, re-appointed on the accession of George III
1802	George (Capel), Earl of Essex
1817	John Somers Cocks, 1st Earl Somers
1841	William Bateman, 1st Baron Bateman
1845	John Somers Cocks, 2nd Earl Somers
1852	William Bateman-Hanbury, 2nd Baron Bateman
1902	John Hungerford Arkwright
1904	Sir John Cotterell, 4th baronet
1933	Arthur Somers Cocks, 6th Baron Somers
1945	Sir Richard Cotterell, 5th baronet

1957	James Thomas, 1st Viscount Cilcennin
1960	John Francis Maclean
1974–98	Hereford & Worcester Lieutenancy
1998	Sir Thomas Dunne
2008–	Lady Darnley

(Sources: Duncumb 1804 (*sic*), Herefordshire Council and others)

MAYORS OF HEREFORD (PART 2)

Established by a Charter of Richard II, the Bailiff of Hereford became mayor, subject to annual election. Those in office at the beginning of each monarchical reign (up to and including Victoria) were listed as follows:

Date	Mayor	Monarch
1382	Thomas Whitfield	Richard II
1399	Thomas Chippenham	Henry IV
1413	John Mey	Henry V
1422	John Falke	Henry VI
1461	John Vintner	Edward IV
1483	John Stockton (d.) /	Richard III
	John Chippenham	
1485	Thomas Mey	Henry VII
1509	Richard Phillips	Henry VIII
1547	Rowland Meece	Edward VI
1553	William Smooth	Mary
1559	Thomas Gibbs	Elizabeth I
1603	John Midson	James I
1625	Richard Veynoll	Charles I
1649	Thomas Seaborne	Charles II
1685	Griffiths Reynolds	James II
1689	Thomas Clark / Henry Smith	William & Mary
1702	Charles Carwardine	Anne
1715	Thomas Paynard	George I
1728	Thomas Ford	George II
1760	Richard Moore	George III
1820	William Pateshall	George IV
1829	James Eyre	William IV
1837	Jonathan Elliott Gough	Victoria

Councillor Charles Nicholls (2015–16) is Hereford's 634th mayor!

MAYORS OF ELSEWHERE

Kington elects its mayor annually: the current (2016) is Councillor Mrs Elizabeth Banks. Two deputy mayors are the immediate past and the immediate next. **Bromyard, Ross, Leominster** and **Ledbury** also have mayors.

HEREFORDSHIRE PLACES CONSIDERED TOWNS (IN C. 1805)

Bromyard	Kington	Orleton
Dorstone	Ledbury	Pembridge
Hereford	Leominster	Ross
Kingsland	Longtown	Weobl[e]y

NINETEENTH-CENTURY ADMIN

There were eleven Herefordshire Hundreds in the nineteenth century:

Broxash, Euras (Ewyas) Lacy, Gremworth, Greytree, Huntingdon, Ludlow, Stretford, Webtree, Wigmore, Woolphy and Wormelow.

Within these sat some 221 parishes, incorporating one city (Hereford), two borough towns (Leominster and Weobl[e]y), and five other market towns (Ledbury, Ross-on-Wye, Kington, Pembridge and Bromyard).

MODERN GOVERNMENT

In more modern times, Herefordshire the administrative county was established under the Local Government Act of 1888. In 1974, it became a combined authority with Worcester but, in 1998, reverted to the unitary authority it remains today.

Since the eleventh century, Herefordshire has also been a ceremonial or shrieval county. Every March a Lord Lieutenant – the monarch's representative in the county – and a High Sheriff are appointed through the ancient ritual 'pricking the vellum'. Here the nation's ruler pricks a hole alongside the name of the successful candidate, using a ceremonial bodkin instead of an erasable pen. Said to originate as a means of denying the unhappy victor an easy way out!

THE CHANGING FACE OF HEREFORDSHIRE

From the Saxons to modernity, the movement of people has shaped and re-shaped the county and, no doubt, numbers will continue to rise and fall as they have throughout its cosmopolitan history.

Herefordshire's population at Domesday was 4,453 – broken down as follows:

Villeins (villagers)	1,730
Bordars	1,271
Serfs (servants)	739
Oxmen	142
Men	134
King's Men	96
Miscellaneous*	341
TOTAL	4,453

*includes Welshmen, Freemen, Reeves, Sergeants and Carpenters

(Source: www.herefordshire.gov.uk)

One interpretation sees the majority of the county's population 'following the plough', a peak in numbers frequently found at settlements with the highest number of teams (oxen). Such was the importance of agriculture to the Herefordshire people.

The following is sourced from Herefordshire Council's 'Facts and Figures' reports (www.herefordshire.gov.uk):

Today (as of 2011), the county's population exceeds 183,000, an exponential rise by any measure.

Between 1831 and 1881, the number rose from 111,000 to just 121,000, and by the turn of the century, actually *fell*, to 116,000. The industrial revolution, which accounted for rocketing numbers in the cities and towns, cannot be easily attributed to a county with such a rural economy.

More recently, the numbers perhaps show the effect of global migration, with a seasonal demand for agricultural labour being met by workers from other parts of the world. Between 2011 and 2012, the population grew more than 1%, and by 2031 is predicted to reach 205,000, a *c.* 17% growth since the end of the previous millennium.

The county has a higher proportion, 22%, of people aged sixty-five or more, compared to a national average of just 17%. Nearly 6,000 people are octogenarians or older, while the age of young people (under twenty years old) has *fallen*, with Leominster, Credenhill, south Hereford and Ross-on-Wye losing the lion's share. Indeed, the county loses approximately 1,000 under-25s every year – owing, it is claimed, to a paucity of work and a lack of University campus [though see Chapter 9].

The county's ethnic complexion is, and was, especially diverse. Mobile communities, including gypsies and Irish Travellers, have remained a substantial part of the Herefordshire 'family'.

IN THIS YEAR ...

Some (random) dates from Herefordshire's history, most of them featured elsewhere in this book. Some are of local importance, others national, still more *inter*national:

Date	Event
c. 740	**Cuthbert, Bishop of Hereford**, erects a memorial to Milfrith, the King of the Magonsaete, and three other bishops - making Hereford the oldest cathedral city in Western Europe
1055	**Gruffydd ap Llywelyn** ravages Hereford, destroying its castle, cathedral and most of the town – 'leaving nothing in the town but blood and ashes, and the walls razed to the ground'
1107–58	Construction of the **Romanesque (Norman) Hereford Cathedral**, much of which can be seen to this day
1138	**Stephen crowns himself king** at Hereford Cathedral, while first the city is burned below the town bridge and later the suburbs on the far side of the Wye
1189	**Richard I's charter** to the people of Hereford
1217	**New Magna Carta** The original great document of civil rights and liberties, signed by King John in 1215. Two years later, after the death of the king and civil war for now quashed, the new child king, Henry III, re-distributed the charter in an updated form. One of only four copies to survive remains in Hereford Cathedral, some eight centuries years on

1326	**The oldest surviving dovecote** in Britain is erected at Garway
1461	**Battle of Mortimer's Cross** near Leominster is a pivotal moment in the Wars of the Roses
1609	Hereford's famed **hobbie-horse race** and **May Morris Daunce** draws thousands of spectators from near and far
1641	The surviving, famed **Monnington Walk** (1 mile of Scotch firs) is planted by newly elected MP, Sir Thomas Tomkins of Monnington Court
1645	Earl Leven leads his Scots army to their famed **siege of Hereford city**. Camped outside the walls for six weeks, their failed attempts to breech its defences end with a major retreat when faced with the king and his forces from Worcester
1715	The **Three Choirs Festival** is (conjectured) to start
1786	On Easter Monday, the entire **West End of Hereford Cathedral collapses**. Wyatt's renovations draw unfavourable views
1802	**Lord Horatio Nelson** is made an honorary Hereford Freeman. During his regional tour with Lady Emma Hamilton, he visits the Swan Inn, Ross-on-Wye, the City Arms Hotel, Hereford, Downton Castle and Pencombe, where he meets the incumbent, his godfather, the Reverend Herbert Glass
1821	**Tom Spring**, bare-knuckle fighter, becomes England's heavyweight champion, a title he retains until 1824
1826	Inaugural **Herefordshire Bow Meeting** is held at Hampton Court Castle, an iconic festival that occurs to this day
1845	The **canals** reach Hereford in May 1845
1853	The coming of the **railways** is celebrated in Hereford on 6 December. Some 60,000 people descend on the town for an array of festivities
1903	William Haywood is the last person **hanged at Hereford Gaol**
1916	**Eight schoolgirls are killed** in a disastrous fire at Hereford's Garrick Theatre, whilst performing a charity concert for First World War soldiers
1924	**Hereford United Football Club** is formed out of St Martin's and Rotherwas

2

HERITAGE I

Herefordshire has a unique collection of historical features. It has the most castles in the UK, and its Iron Age hillforts are some of the best. Yet it has much else besides. From scheduled monuments to rare treasures; bridges to dovecotes; from prehistory to modernity, there's something for everyone interested in this county's unparalleled past.

Note: The listings below can be used as a gazetteer of samples, or as a simple introduction to Herefordshire's glorious past. Much of the information is informed by Herefordshire Council's Historic Environment Record (HER) and/or Historic England's National Heritage List for England (NHLE). Each entry quotes the relevant 'asset number' in the form HER#, NHLE#, for future reference. See bibliography for respective websites.

MONUMENTS

(Note: Offa's Dyke has its own entry – see Chapter 4)

According to Historic England, Herefordshire has almost 100 scheduled monuments, protected in law against unlawful damage and harm. From a selection of a staggering 23,000 heritage 'sites' (see also Buildings, p.28) here is a sample of just some of the best:

Arthur's Stone, Dorstone (1528, 1010720) – Neolithic stone burial chamber, perched high on Merbach Hill. Built in the Cotswold–Severn style, having side chambers. What remains is an evocative blend of fallen stone, surviving chamber and suggestions of the central passage deep into the tomb. The eponymous Arthur's Stone, a large, prostrate slab seen in the nearby ditch, may be part of the original structure.

Credenhill Camp (906, 1005526) – Iron Age hillfort, on a site easily recognisable for miles around. Occupied *c.* 390 BCE–75 ACE, it has at least three entrances (the fourth may be modern). With only one defensive rampart, it is a good example of the univallate ringfort style; others nearby include Sutton Walls and Aconbury. An inner bank soars almost 9m high. The camp was later annexed by both the Roman military and by the wider medieval landscape.

British Camp (aka Herefordshire Beacon Camp), Colwall (932, 1001792) – another fine Herefordshire hillfort, straddling two hills high up in the Malverns. It retains the colossal bank and ditch on all sides. Built during the Iron Age, it was augmented in the early medieval and medieval periods. A defined ringwork, nicknamed The Citadel, lies within, and possibly dates to the tenth century. Note also Shire Ditch (3823, 1003812), a medieval boundary dyke, running on the south-eastern side.

Magna, Kenchester (121, 1001768) – Romano-British small town of *Magna* (modern Kenchester). Occupation on the site began in the first century and lasted till well into the fifth. It is defined today by its clear scarp. Mosaics (seen at Hereford Museum), hypocausts, even cremations reveal this as one of Herefordshire's most important Roman centres known today. Scapula possibly launched his raids into Wales from here.

Bravonium and **Jay Lane,** Leintwardine (549, 1005522; 578, 1005367) – Roman town and fort of *Bravonium* and associated military station known as *Bravinium* [*sic*]. Relatively uncommon features, these smaller encampments provided essential men and supplies into the central Marches. Typically used during the first and second centuries ACE, these remained active well into the fourth.

Hereford City Walls, Rampart and Ditch (20249, 1005528) – defined as the 'wall surrounding the whole medieval city, including several bastion … ramparts and ditches'. Originally the Mercian town of Hereford ('army ford'), it was first enclosed in *c.* eighth/ninth century by constructing a simple earth bank and ditch. King Alfred strengthened and enlarged it late in the ninth (for example, to include *St Guthlac's*, now Castle Green). The eleventh-century 'new town' to the north of this old Saxon *burh* (or fortified centre) – which it gradually subsumed – flourished after the charter of 1189. It was then Richard I sold the town to its people in exchange for maintaining its defences. In the thirteenth century a ring of stone was constructed, which included six gates and some seventeen towers.

MUSEUMS

Herefordshire museums provide an array of
rare treasures, defining both the county's
past and its latter-day life. Included
here are specialist museums,
including one devoted to cider
and another to science fiction
and the famed *Dr Who*! Please
check opening times etc. before
visiting. This list is by no
means exhaustive.

Hereford Museum and Art Gallery

Housed in a splendid
Victorian Gothic building,
the museum opened in
1874. Its collection includes: a
pair of percussion duelling pistols,
made *c.* 1860 by Baker's of Hereford;
an Ethelred the Unready silver penny, dated to
the late tenth/early eleventh century and minted
in Hereford; an Early Bronze Age crouched burial discovered in
the Olchon Valley; a seventeenth-century marriage quilt made
of quilted and embroidered silk satin; and a Saxon enamelled
reliquary mount, found in the area of the old Welsh *commote*,
Archenfield. Undoubtedly, though, the prize in its collection is the
Kenchester (*Magna*) Roman mosaic, which hangs on the stairwell
near the front door. A timeline steers you around the museum.

The Cider Museum, Hereford

Housed in a former cider-making factory, the story of Herefordshire's
most famous industry is re-told through exhibits, word and sound.
Visit for a sensory indulgence of all things decidedly apple!

Butcher Row House Museum, Ledbury

From Civil War armour to a Tibetan pipe, local pottery to black and
white prints, this local museum highlights life in Ledbury as it used to be
lived. It is located in the Butcher Row House, a rare survivor of a medieval
row that once ran along the middle of the modern-day High Street, but
which was rebuilt on a new site tucked away down Church Lane.

Kington Museum

A museum in the heart of Drover Country (see p.28), its collection captures life from this ancient settlement right through to the town of today. The museum proudly houses the remains of Daisy (or Nellie?), Kington's very own elephant, who died suddenly in 1932: she had neared the end of an arduous walk from Leominster, advertising the old Chapman's Circus, when tragedy struck. Her bones were rediscovered fifty-six years later, although her legend then, as now, has never been lost.

Leominster Museum

An eclectic hoard of artefacts and ephemera from Leominster and its environs. From the Romans to religion, conquest to farming, its treasures illuminate the history of this ancient and venerable town. World events and personal stories are told through the words and belongings of those who have gone amongst us before.

Time Machine Museum of Science Fiction, Bromyard

A modern spin on the traditional museum, this delve into sci-fi and monsters is a must for all lovers of *Dr Who*, *Star Trek*, *Thunderbirds* and shows of a similar ilk. Housed in the heart of this historic wool town, it transports you to another dimension where the future and past dramatically collide.

Weobley Museum

Weobley life and personalities are revealed in one of Herefordshire's smallest and most charming museums, located in this prized black-and-white town (see p.108). From the history of Weobley Castle, assailed by Stephen during The Anarchy wars, reflections on the Great War, to tales of folklore and myth, this is a place for learning more about life in this, the 'lea belonging to Webba'.

BUILDINGS

Amidst the many fine buildings in Herefordshire, almost 2,000 are listed for their architectural splendour, historical significance, or a union of both. Those listed Grade I are outstanding, while many regardless of class are of particular note. Still others can only be described as ... fantastically odd.

The following examples are found in the NHLE (see above). Note: many more, including bridges, churches, stately homes, even milestones, feature throughout the book.

Unless stated, please assume sites mentioned are *not* open to the public, though many can be seen from public spaces. Check access (if any) before travelling.

Six Buildings Listed Grade I

College of Vicars Choral, *off Cathedral Close, Hereford*
An ecclesiastical college, built *c.* 1473, a replacement for the one granted under charter from Richard II (1395). Built largely of local sandstone, the centre quadrangle is surrounded by the vicars' cloisters. The porch of the college, of a similar date, retains the original oak door and postern. Ceasing to be a college in the twentieth century, it was originally intended to house twenty-seven vicars choral, obliged to attend (intone) cathedral services and provide singing voices for the absent canons. A covered walkway, known as St John's Walk, or Little Cloister, connected the college to the south-east transept of the cathedral. In 2015 it underwent extensive restoration for the first time in 150 years.

Ruins of Wilton Castle, Ross-on-Wye *(open certain days of the year)* **and House** *(not open to the public)*
Established on the banks of the River Wye, this fourteenth-century castle (a scheduled monument) and the ruinous sixteenth-century house (not open to the public) capture both the violent and romantic histories of the county's past. They are built largely of red sandstone and tufa (calcium carbonate).

Hellens Manor, *Much Marcle (open certain days of the year)*
One of the oldest dwellings in England, this Elizabethan manor house with much older foundations has suffered several reductions in size. It nonetheless remains much as it was in the reign of King Charles I. The Hellens estate includes a dovecote – fashioned from the tower of the old castle that once stood nearby – and a very fine cider house. Its history owes much to royal visits and historic events. Anne Boleyn, Bloody Queen Mary, Elizabeth I, all have a connection. More than two centuries earlier, Queen Isabella is said to have waited at Hellens for the Great Seal of England, which she secured with Roger Mortimer and the removal of her husband, King Edward II. In all, Hellens remains one of Herefordshire's most significant – and perhaps least known – historic houses.

Pembridge Castle, *Welsh Newton*

Once a castle, now a private farmhouse, on the English–Welsh border, it was built from the late twelfth/early thirteenth century onwards, and has seventeenth-century domestic outbuildings. The castle was significantly ruined in 1644 while it served as an outpost for the Royalists of Monmouth. It was substantially restored in the twentieth century. (Note: private)

Dovecot *(about 80yd south-east of the Church of St Michael, Garway)*

This fourteenth century dovecot is the oldest known survivor of its particular class – round with a squat base. The original entrance is contemporary but a later doorway (nineteenth century) has since been inserted. Contains some nineteen nesting holes from which the *squabs* (chicks) were taken (see Chapter 14).

Holme Lacy House, *Holme Lacy*

A seventeenth-century country house (now an hotel) with later amendments. The main façade once contained thirteen bays but has now been largely extended. It still has the original seventeenth-century plastered ceilings, panelling and Corinthian pilastered hall.

Six Listed Buildings of Particular Interest

Entrance gatehouse to the Butter Market, *Hereford*

Visible from the heart of Hereford's High Town, the entrance gatehouse to the Butter Market can easily escape the notice of a hurrying shopper. Yet it has much to marvel: keystone with figure, a central frieze with figures to side, a bellcote with weather vane and clock tower, the timepiece of which was made by J. Smith & Sons, steam works in Derby. The whole thing was built *c.* 1860 by John Clayton.

Goff's Endowed Day School and United Reformed Church, *Huntington*

Former school and adjoining Congregational Chapel, it is now a United Reformed Church. Built in the late eighteenth century (the date stone reads 1791), it served as a non-conformist establishment established by Edward Goff, a coal merchant of Scotland Yard, London. The former church joins to the rear of the school.

The Master's House of St Katherine's Hall, *Ledbury (see also p.105)*

Although this fifteenth century hospital is now surrounded by post-medieval neighbours, much of the Master's House remains as it did the day it was built. Historic England record it as 'a rare and almost unique example of a building type which was once commonly associated with hospital and infirmary sites' (NHLE). The Victoria County History project refer to the Master's House as 'a late example of a medieval hall house because in Herefordshire after about 1500 the preference was to build ceiled halls, with chimneystacks rather than an open hearth' (Victoria County History (VCA)). The building now houses council offices and amenities, having recently undergone extensive restoration with a focus on public interpretation.

It was originally a single storey hall, with two-storeyed cross wings at either end. The one to the west incorporated the *solar* (private quarters), while the other (east) housed the pantry and more. Much of the old timber framing is once again visible (or known to lie beneath wallpaper), while original fifteenth-century wainscoting has been returned to some of the rooms. Four oriel windows (bay windows projecting from the wall but detached from the ground) shed light on the eighteenth-century staircase; while from the ground floor the original roof can be seen once more (the recently removed upper storey was a late insert). Various styles of strut, braces, tie beams and purlins provide a rare tableau of medieval architectural life. There is only one other surviving master's house of a medieval hospital in the country.

Nine Listed 'Oddities'
Clodock Sundial, *St Clydog's church, Longtown*
For those interested in gnomons, solar clocks and the earth's polar axis, a stepped plinth and ashlar shaft carries an eighteenth-century sundial, positioned some metres to the south of the church. In use long before mechanical timepieces, local time held sway according to publicly located sundials and an appreciation of the sun's orbit. Simple in their execution, the science behind these early 'smart watches' was intricate and profound. Indeed, when early train timetables were standardised in 1847, the new (mechanical) clocks were calibrated by reference to sundials such as this!

Eywood Ice House, *Titley*
A circular, domed, eighteenth-century ice house, with entrance to the east. It once served Eywood – itself demolished in the mid-twentieth century – while the estate is maintained as a registered garden and park. It was visited in 1812 by the Romantic poet Lord Byron, who enjoyed an affair with its mistress, Lady Oxford. The estate is not open to the public.

Coffin Lids, *Tedstone Delamare*
A pair of thirteenth-century coffin lids, in the churchyard of St James, situated south-west of the porch. Each is adorned with a man's head, foliage and a trefoil surround.

Obelisk, *Eastnor Park*

This nineteenth-century obelisk sits 240m above sea level in the resplendent Eastnor Park. Erected in 1812 for the 2nd Lord Somers, inscriptions appear on panels fixed near the base on all four of its sides. One, on the north face, commemorates the 'Honourable Edward Cocks', who died in that year, while fighting in Spain. On the east, 'Lord Chancellor Somers' is commemorated, who died six years earlier, while the southern face remembers a long-lost James Cocks, Ensign, who departed this life in 1758. Listed Grade II*.

Ruined House, *Stapleton Castle*

This ruinous seventeenth-century house on the site of thirteenth-century Stapleton Castle was once the home of several worthies, including the Says, Mortimers and Harleys. Built of sandstone and brick, its dilapidated state retains parts of a fireplace and windows, the whole visible from a nearby public right of way. Last occupied *c.* 1870. (See RCHM, Herefordshire, Vol. III, p. 182; *Burke's and Savills Guide to Country Houses*, 1980, p. 57.)

Friends' Meeting House, *Almeley*

A black-and-white, timber-framed meeting house constructed in 1672 and greatly restored in the mid-twentieth century. It has a half-hipped roof, plaster walls (infill) and was built on a sandstone base; its interior includes a single truss and staircase up to half-length gallery. The door is reputed to be seventeenth century, having strap hinges and a timber porch. The stone stack on the outside incorporates a baking oven. The meeting house was founded in the seventeenth century by one Roger Pritchard.

Hergest Croft Granary, *Kington (gardens open)*

Formally the solar wing to a hall house attached to Hergest Court, it has fourteenth-century origins with later additions.

St Peter's Church Cross, *Rowlestone*

A rare fifteenth-century stone cross with nineteenth-century shaft – a rare survivor of ecclesiastical history from the Middle Ages. Inscription remembers a former cleric.

Range of Barns, *Burghill*

Part of Burghill Manor, this range of barns dates from the seventeenth/ eighteenth century. It has five bays, a stable and loft, and a further seven-bayed barn at right angles to the others. A threshing floor and trusses survive in the interior. Not open to the public but apparently visible from the road.

LANDSCAPE ARCHAEOLOGY

The county's landscape is both sprawling and, so it seems, largely unchanged. But it has altered, and many of its memories have been lost to the ravages of time.

In the fields around Weston-under-Penyard, a once thriving hubbub of Roman occupation commanded the lands to the east of the Wye. *Ariconium* was above all else an industrial centre, smelting ore from the Forest of Dean (and no doubt equipping the armies in their fight with the Welsh). Blackened soil, so often a feature of these Roman sites, defines the land against its more usual red; as do the bloomeries, furnaces and nuggets of slag (*scoriae*), all revealed by the plough. It was lost long before 1066 but its memory possibly survives in the name of the old British (Welsh) enclave, *Arcenfelde* (Archenfield) which, it is claimed, emerged from the embers of Roman control.

LIME KILNS

Kilns, which once peppered the county, were where lime was extracted for building or enriching the land. With the Normans came new buildings of stone and, with them, a new demand through the use of lime mortar. Many survive in a ruinous state, others as earthworks. Of the 270 recorded in Herefordshire, here are two of the best:

Craswall (220m west of Llan Oleu) – This is a handsome example of a limekiln site, possibly in use over a long, drawn-out period (some were used only the once). Visible from the Offa's Dyke path, it is located near a footpath to the north. Its association with a pair of Bronze Age round barrows –  which the kiln impedes – only adds to the mystique. Unsurprisingly, it is a scheduled monument.

Leintwardine – this is a superb restored example, visible on the side of the A4113 to the north. It is located on the left, north-east of Kinton. It was built in the late eighteenth/early nineteenth century, with a triple arch, and stands approximately 6ft high. A second kiln stands nearby to the east. Both are Grade II listed.

3

ENVIRONMENT

Often for good, sometimes for ill, Herefordshire's environment has been at the heart of its fortunes …

Its geology rips the county in two, so that each side must farm necessarily different. Yet, despite its poor soil and a much cooler climate, innovation has proved the mother of progress. From advances in irrigation to the importance of 'new' crops, its fortunes have risen equally on the backs of its beasts … from the famed Hereford Bull to the renowned Ryeland sheep. Along with its apples and pears (and latterly soft fruits), Herefordshire has a legitimate claim to be the nation's food growing centre.

GEOGRAPHY

From the Malverns in the east, to the contested borderlands of the west, from the slopes of the Black Mountains to the Teme in the north, Herefordshire's varied and vivid geography is seen in both the form and titles of its natural wonders.

Valleys
Cusop Valley (Dingle) – once (still?) the only place in the county to see the Mountain Vetch (*Vicia Orobus*) and Creeping Willow (*Salix repens*)

Fownhope Valley – once a particular haven for the humble hedgehog

Frome Valley

Golden Valley – the home of the *Stradelei* (see 'Domesday'), described by Kilvert as beholding its 'quaint picturesque old-fashioned farm houses'

Grwyne Valley – containing just six isolated miles of rural Herefordshire

Lugg Valley – along with the Wye, home of the otter

Monnow Valley – once the exclusive habitat of the slow worm lizard

(*Anguis fragilis*) and the inappropriately named (in these parts) Common or Ringed Snake (*Tropidonotus natrix*)

Olchon Valley – with its prehistoric archaeology and timeless appeal

Severn Valley

Teme Valley

Wigmore Valley

Woolhope 'Valley of Elevation' – so-called for its geological history that produced an astonishing arena of valleys and ridges in the east of the county

Wye Valley – hosting the great Right of Way

'Cockshoots' – Herefordshire name for incipient valleys punctuating outcrops of rock

Hills

Aconbury

Cat's Back, in Herefordshire's Black Mountains

Credenhill – densely wooded and home to the great Iron Age hillfort

Dinedor

Dinmore and its vast forest

Doward Hills – with King Arthur's Cave and Merlin's Cave, two fancifully named natural features, producing evidence of early human occupation over some 25,000 years

Garway – home to the small red viper and the Slow-worm, or Blindworm lizard (*Anguis fragilis*)

Moccas and Merbach, with their (private) woodland and (accessible) common, respectively

Saddlebow

The Pyons, especially the prominent, eponymous Pyon Hill

Tyberton

… And finally, the fantastically named **Lady Lift** and **Robin Hood's Butts**

Commons

Bircher, near Yarpole	Gorsley	Swinmore*
Bromyard	Hurstway	Upper Grove
Byford	Kyre	Vowchurch
Durlow (Durley)	Meer	Widemarsh†
Ewyas Harold	Peterstow	
Ferney	Putley	

* relic name of Moccas (swine-moor, *moccas* being Welsh for pig)
† beyond Hereford, lost long ago – claimed as the site where John Kemble (later St John) was hung, drawn and quartered (see p.162)

GEOLOGY

Ice! So much ice. Sheets, floes and glaciers first imprisoned then shaped the county we know today. Before 10,000 BP, it descended 200m into the ground, while even in the Mesolithic (*c.* 8,000–4,000 BCE) the western reaches as far east as what is now Hereford lay waste beneath its frozen grasp.

When the thaw did come, a sea some 11,000ft deep inundated the land. Rivers formed, most notably the Wye, which shaped and scoured the ridges and valleys that give the county today its timeless appeal.

However, scholarly discord has not yet confirmed what happened next. Melting ice formed a lake, or was it a bay? But whichever the case, Herefordshire became a natural amphitheatre of water, surrounded by peaks.

Over eons of time, the rocks underneath shattered and broke, producing rose-coloured earth and a tilth sprinkled with stone, as well as:

- A soil so rich in colour that the rain turns the lanes into rivers of chocolate
- 'Old Red Sandstone', to a depth of 10,000ft, which has defined large parts of the county and its architectural style
- Gravels and shales, which have brought wealth to the quarries
- Cornstone, which is hauled and burnt into lime (though of variable grade)

Fossils

Even the sterile Old Red has produced astonishing Herefordshire fossils – lithic remains of a pre-glacial life. The giant sea creature, Eurypterida (*Pterygotus taurinus*), measuring 7ft long; a 3ft-long scorpion (*Praearcturus gigas*); and the largest fish spine ever recovered (*Onchus major*) have all been discovered in Herefordshire.

The Rowlestone Beds, though, have failed to produce coal (fossilised vegetation), despite the county sharing its border with the Forest of Dean.

Earthquakes

It might be a surprise that Herefordshire has suffered several earthquakes! On 6 October 1863, the county gaol was damaged and would have collapsed but for iron braces recently fitted. A second, on 17 December 1896, led to reports of stopped clocks, books that moved on the shelf and chimneys that crashed to the ground. A more recent event, in 2008, centred on Bromyard, and measured 3.6 on the Richter scale.

Mountain High, River Deep

In a county defined by its mountains, hills, rivers and streams, the following facts and recollections cement their natural awe:

Black Mountains

Forming part of the Brecon Beacons National Park (Wales), this natural border between the Angle and Celt stretches from Cusop in the north-west to Ewyas Vale and on to the south-east – a distance of some 30 or so miles.

The slopes, in truth, form a primordial pyramid, triangulating Abergavenny, Hay-on-Wye and down to Llangors. Viewed from the relative calm of the Golden Valley, it is easy to see how the range got its name. Inhospitable in any month of the year, to walk them is to enter nature in all her terrible force.

The diarist (and fantasist?) the Reverend Kilvert found wonder and inspiration from a range he considered Heaven on earth:

> [In the snow] the mountains stood up in the clear blue heaven, a long rampart line of dazzling glittering snow so as no fuller on earth can white them. I stood rooted to the ground, struck with amazement and overwhelmed at the extraordinary splendour of this marvellous spectacle. I never saw anything to equal it I think, even among the high Alps. (Plomer, 1944: p.112)

The snow played its part in another illusion, turning the Black Mountains into proof of God's might:

> I stopped and turned to look at the view. I saw what I thought was a long dazzling white and golden cloud up in the sky. Suddenly I found that I had been gazing at the great snow slopes of the Black Mountain lit up by the setting sun and looking through the dark storm clouds. It was a sublime spectacle, the long white rampart dazzling in its brilliancy and warmed by a golden tinge standing high up above the clear dark line of the nearer hills taking the sunshine, and bathed in glory. Then in the silence the Hay Church bell for evensong boomed suddenly out across the valley. (Plomer, 1944: pp.167–68)

Rivers

Herefordshire is blessed – and, during flood, unequivocally cursed – by some of the nation's longest, most revered rivers. Collectively, they define the county, and perhaps this is why so many are now joined by a National Trail or public right of way.

Wye – first languishing then meandering, and eventually careering, the 'Oh! Sylvan Wye' (Wordsworth, *Lyrical Ballads*, 1798) runs for 134 miles, from Plynlimon in the Welsh mountains down to Chepstow and on to the sea. Famously tidal, though only in part (below the aptly named Bigsweir Bridge), further upstream it glides effortlessly by. Forming a natural border between England and Wales (and vice versa!), it once formed an unimpeachable part of King Offa's dyke (see p.54).

At various points, commercial and leisure trades have burst forth (see Chapter 11), while in 2004–05 it became the first major river to be made a Site of Special Scientific Interest (SSSI) – see below.

Tributaries

The Wye's command of the county is such that the following – directly or indirectly – become part of its source:

Lugg – arrives into Herefordshire at Rosser's Bridge, north-east of Combe, trickling in from Wales via Llangunllo and Presteigne. Along its 45 miles, it serves the priory town of Leominster, and a host of smaller settlements, before discharging into the Wye near Mordiford Bridge (see p.169). Its importance to local life is captured in several place names: Moreton-on-Lugg, Lugwardine, Lugg Green, Lugharness and even Lucton.

Arrow – running (roughly) east–west, it's easy to see how the river acquired its name. From Glascwm in Powys, to just south of Leominster, it arcs past a quiver of settlements, many of which have absorbed more than simply its water – Michaelchurch-on-Arrow (in Wales), Staunton-on-Arrow (not to be confused with Staunton-on-Wye), Arrow Green ... Its key characteristic though is in its being a tributary of the Lugg (the two converging below Stoke Prior), making it a secondary tributary of the great Wye.

Monnow – originating in Craswall on the slopes below the Black Mountains, only the first few miles lie within Herefordshire. It leaves the county (and country) south of Clodock, while its chief settlement, Monmouth, recognises the Welsh source of its name – *Mynwy*, or swift water.

Dore – a tributary of the Monnow, its course in the south-west of the county (Cusop) gave its name to the famed Golden Valley. Believed to be a Norman corruption of its more likely Welsh name, *dûr*, bastardised into *d'Or*, the French term meaning quite literally, '[valley] of gold'. Its most recognised point must be Dore Abbey, the twelfth-century Cistercian abbey from which the village has since taken its name (see p.163).

Frome – a tributary of the Lugg (and thus of the Wye, just a few miles farther on), it flows south-west from its source north of Bromyard, past Yarkhill, before arriving in Hampton Bishop. Several settlements have adopted its name, where it meanders on by: the Frome of Bishop's, Canon, Prior's and Castle.

Garron – a smaller, often forgotten waterway in the south-east of the county, discharging into the Wye at Whitchurch near that place's tremendous oxbows around Symonds Yat.

Also: the Clun, Kenwater, Leadon (Leddon), Redlake, Teme and countless others rivers, brooks and streams all course through the county, producing source waters and tributaries to the rivers above.

HOPS, CROPS, APPLES AND PEARS

Draw a line down the middle of the county, and its divided conditions meant finding good pasture in the east was as rare as good crops in the west. And only then to a very low standard (poor quality grazing in the west, and stunted crops to the east, the clay soils holding the water and making roots perish in cold clods of earth). Things, though, eventually changed with fresh practices, machinery and, lately, new crops.

Farming in Herefordshire had an unpromising start. Poor conditions – climate, land, even labour – and its rigid adherence to the old 'open strip' system, all hindered progress. Ploughing was hard, with two out of every three years left fallow. The overwintering of stock became an unrealised dream.

With enclosure came eviction, so that late eighteenth-century farming 'advances' proved as unpopular as the earlier starvation caused by unpromising crops.

Even the county's ox numbers were worryingly low and its sheep typically small. Great tracts of land remained 'waste', a relic of the Welsh border incursions. And though livestock successes would bring temporary cheer, it was other crops, out of season and fashion, which rescued the agrarian wealth. Such were the 'cash crops' of hops, orchards … and drink.

Hops

Commercial growing of hops flourished with the demand for better, more affordable ale. Properly called beer (old English ale used only malt), Dutch labourers working in England imported their preferred 'hoppy brew' during the 1500s. Though the hop was already in England since before Edward I, its greatest appeal had not yet emerged. Indeed, in the face of such Dutch pressure, Parliament was petitioned to wipe out this renowned 'wicked weed'. All that would change.

It surprises many to learn that well into the twentieth century the hop growing capital of England was not Kent or Worcester, but Hereford county! Here, 100 years before, 7,000 acres of cultivar hops were being regularly worked. The eastern half of the shire accounted for most, as they exploited better marls and alluvial (river) silts from the Wye, Lugg and Teme. Indeed, they had perfect growing conditions: 'It is said that the land by the Teme will grow hops for ever' (Whitehead 1893).

Hop money came pouring into the county. However, such was its new popularity with the farmers, that it inevitably brought other, imminent despair. So much land had been 'stolen' from more nourishing crops, that Herefordshire people might well end up wealthy and drunk, but they were also about to die of starvation.

Herefordshire hops, like grapes – whose names they sometimes adopt – were categorised into red and white types. By the close of the 1700s, all were held 'in the highest estimation'.

White

- The Golden Vine, a white hop with a red vine
- Cooper's White, an excellent hop 'lately introduced'
- The Farnham White lately introduced from Farnham
- The Kentish Grape
- The Mathon White
- The Townend Green wired hop, 'a remarkably large square hop first grown at Townend in the parish of Bosbury'

Red
- The Red Vine or Chester red.
- The Newcombe
(Source: VCH 1908)

Growing Tips For 'A Perfite Platforme of a Hoppe Garden'
(from Reynold Scott's *Arte of Gardening*, 1574)

> If your ground be grasse, it should be first sowen with hempe
> or beanes which maketh the ground melowe destroyeth weedes,
> and leaveth the same in good season for this purpose. At the
> end of Marche, repayre to some good garden to compound
> with the owner for choice rootes which in some places will cost
> 5d an hundreth. And now you must choose the biggest rootes
> you can find such as are three or four inches about, and let every
> roote be nine or ten inches long.

Holes were to be dug at least 8ft apart, 1ft square, 1ft deep, and in each
two or three roots planted, and well 'hilled' up. Three or four poles 'at
the most' were to be set to each hill, 15 or 16ft long 'except [if] your
ground be very rich'. The poles should be 9 or 10in in circumference
at the butt, so that 'they shall endure the longer and stand the wind
better'. After they were put in, the earth round the poles should be
well rammed. The hops tied with rushes or grass. During the growth
of the hops, not more than two or three 'stalks' being allowed per pole,
after the first year the hills were gradually to be raised from the alleys
between the rows, thus giving the ground a good stirring, so that the
greater 'you make your hylles the more hoppes you shall have upon
your poales'. (Based on VCH 1908: pp 422–3)

Orchard Fruits
Though many sites had been lost to the hop, new
apples and pears – more particularly, cider and
perry – contributed to Herefordshire's reputation
for being a county of 'verdant orchards'. And, by
the start of the Restoration, it had already gained it
reputation as 'the orchard of England'.

Cider (see also Chapter 10)
Cider was a man's drink: strong, full bodied and heavy! So claimed a
voice in the past.

The apples most frequently favoured included the renowned Red Streak, Gennet Moyle, Stire and the Bromsbery Crab. The smaller crab apples, when mixed with 'washings of cider' in the winter made a drink that 'doth well please our day labourers'.

With a reputation spawning such literary works as *Herefordshire Orchards: A Pattern for All England*, the county's produce was in constant demand. Even so, as early as the late eighteenth century, it had failed to arrest the loss of many commendable varieties; and, by the start of the twentieth, numbers were shrinking still further:

Cider	*Table (Dessert)*	*Cooking*
Foxwhelp	Ribston Pippin	Keswick
Red Cowarne	Golden Pippin	Codlin
Hagloe Crab	King Pippin	Wellington
Brandy Apple	Cox's Orange Pippin	Lord Suffield
Cockagee	Margel	Collins
Stire	Court of Wick	Alfreston
Dymmock Red	Blenheim Orange	
Redstreak		
Royal Wilding		
Garter		
Skyrme's Kernel		
Knotted Kernel		
Cherry Norman		
Strawberry Norman		
White Norman		
Cider Lady's Finger		

(Source: VCH 1908 (*sic*))

Perry (Pear Cider)

Perry, on the other hand, was slower to flourish and quicker to fade. In fact, it was originally dismissed for 'breeding wind in the stomack (*sic*)'.

The **Bosbury Pear** – known as the Barland – was a seventeenth-century wonder. Its roots stemmed quite literally from the ancient trees at Hellens, Much Marcle, claimed more than a century before to have been planted in the time of Queen Anne.

Perry	*Dessert*
Taynton Squash	Doyenne d'Eté
Barland	Chaumontel
Huffcap	Cattlac

Oldfield	Williams' Bon Chrétien
Rock Pear	Buerré Diel
Pine Pear	Bergamot
Blakeney Red	Duchesse d'Angoulême
Thorn Pear	Marie Louise

(Source: VCH 1908 (*sic*))

SPUDS, GLORIOUS ... ERM, SWEDES?

On a soil once deemed unsuitable for growing even the humble potato, the harvesting of this familiar tuber has now reached endemic proportions. Large producers of chips, crisps and fries have turned this once infertile land into a rich source of starch-induced wealth.

Herefordshire can also claim (some) credit for the modern popularity of swedes. With other crops failing to germinate or 'fruit', the Swedish turnip gave the county its answer. Known to withstand the cold, wet conditions, it also provided nourishing food for the cattle – and the annual struggle to over-winter the stock.

LIVESTOCK

Hereford Bull – chief among the county's farming achievements was – and still is – the Herefordshire, or Hereford Bull. Slender and light, producing excellent beef, today its value as stud remains exceedingly high. Its origins, though, are shrouded in mystery.

Many hail its beginnings at the time of the Normans, while others prefer to think it came with the Welsh. Lord Scudamore, local worthy and late seventeenth-century farmer, certainly had 'red cows with white faces' imported from Flanders. Meanwhile, mid-eighteenth-century breeders included Benjamin Tomkins of Weobley, Weyman, Yeomans, Hewer and Tulley, all

credited with perfecting the beast. Indeed, since 1788, being well fed and producing good beef ('tender, juicy and fine-grained'), it was often considered 'the first breed of cattle in the land'.

Its greatest appeal, though, came from the work of a number of nineteenth-century breeders, none more so than Thomas Duckham of Holmer. By 1857, he had taken over the herd book and is judged to have been instrumental in its rise to international fame.

Ryeland Sheep – so-called because the land was once thought incapable of growing a grain better than rye – secured an international reputation for quality and high yields of wool. Flocked in large parts of the county, it attracted greatest attention around Leominster, where 'the best wool in England' commanded the top prices per sack.

Golden Valley Sheep, too, at least in the seventeenth century, produced wool described as long and lustrous. Shearing, traditionally done by women, brought reputation and wealth.

GONE FISHING

Owing to its network of rivers, Herefordshire has long had a closer dietary association with fish than many expect so far from the sea. More prevalent in the Middle Ages than modernity, it owed much not least to a scarcity of fresh meat and a far greater number of 'fasting' days that forbade the consumption of flesh.

For those who wished to sell fish to the masses, a toll became due, paid to the Church, sometimes the Crown. The concern of a 'black market' was so great that laws were passed, demanding: 'no one shall meddle with the mystery of fishmongers, except those that belong to it.' Harsh punishments were exacted when even legitimate purveyors were: 'late with your herrings, red and white.'

Locally sourced fish (from the rivers) included eels, sturgeon, lampreys (a jawless, tubular fish), salmon, minnows and trout. Mussels and oysters – then more common than now – were harvested under less stringent conditions.

AND THEN THERE'S ...

In a recent poll (2015), the good people of Herefordshire voted the flower or plant most likely to define their county. They chose ... **mistletoe!**

The 'planted kiss of the year' has, for centuries, been tolerated as a parasite amongst the county's thousands of apples. Now, though, with dwindling orchards and new varieties of apple resistant to its parasitic root (hypocotyl), the humble *Viscum album* faces an uncertain future.

Soft fruits, such as strawberries, raspberries, blackberries and currants are the emergent crop for the new millennium. Armies of foreign labour, coupled with increasing consumer demand, have led to a profusion of crops once never considered part of Herefordshire's agrarian past. Just don't mention the accompanying polytunnels.

NATURAL HISTORY

Bromyard Downs Common attracted recent attention after the accidental discovery of one of nature's rarest visitors to these islands – the **Striped Hawkmoth**. Observed in June 2015, it was only the fourth visit recorded so far inland.

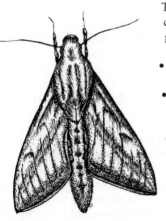

The **little bittern** once favoured the county, but its recent demise is easy to grasp from a sightings report of 1908:

- one shot at Shobdon Court in 1838
- a male specimen in the possession of a Worcestershire man, shot in Herefordshire
- one in the Cardiff Museum, killed over the border at Llangorse Lake

Little wonder it was known for its shy, skulking habits.

The **common bittern** fared even worse:

- one in Hereford Museum, shot at Eastnor Castle (1854)
- one at Backney Marsh shot the same year
- single sightings at Staunton-on-Wye (1861), Staunton Common (1861), Fawley (1879), Sellack (1880) and Dulas (1887) – all shot

One, however, enjoyed greater fortune, last seen alive at the Moor Hay in 1885.

Herefordshire names for the bittern included: miredrum, butterbump, bogbumper, bumpycoss, bull of the bog, bogblutter, and bogjumper!

National Nature Reserves
In light of the previous entry, Herefordshire's wildlife is blessed with three National Nature Reserves (NNRs) – though only one, The Flits, is open to the public (at the time of writing):

The Flits, named after the Old English *fliet*, meaning 'stream', stretches across the floodplain of the Wye, harbouring 200 species of butterflies and moths, as well as rare ferns, bracken and marsh-loving plants. It hosts particular species of less common flies – such as the 'soldier' and 'snail-killer'.

Moccas Park is 'one of the largest and most diverse examples of wood pasture remaining in Britain'. Two hundred species of lichen, rare bats, almost 1,000 species of fly, and much else besides, make this a rare haven for Herefordshire nature.

Downton Gorge is one of the last relics of a Royal Chase, and home to sessile oaks, ash, lime and wych elm. (Source: www.gov.uk 2015)

Areas of Outstanding Natural Beauty
Herefordshire has not one but *two* AONBs, both extending down to the south of the county:

The Wye Valley AONB is the only one in the country (there are some forty-six across the UK, excluding Scotland) to straddle a national border. Running from Mordiford in the north, down to Chepstow in the south, its 128 square miles includes some of the nation's best-loved natural and anthropogenic features. Centuries of farming have long shaped the land. Salmon share its river with kayaks and boats. Its floodplain gives way to resplendent orchards. And a National Trail (Offa's Dyke Path) crosses through, while the Wye Valley Walk enters a gorge (see p.86). In the Wye Valley, Herefordshire possesses one of Britain's most varied and popular landscapes.

Malvern Hills AONB links Herefordshire with the counties of Worcester and Gloucester. In an area renowned for its restorative waters, timeless geology, ancient hillforts and primeval woods, it remains much smaller than its Wye Valley cousin. Roughly 67 square miles across, it engages a total of twenty-two parishes, lying wholly or partly within the AONB. (Note: Its boundary resembles a prowling carp.)

Sites Of Special Scientific Interest
The county boasts some seventy-seven SSSIs, covering both rarities and 'red book' endangered species found in the county. Key sites include the Black Mountains, rivers Lugg, Teme and Wye, parks at Brampton Bryan, Eastnor and Moccas and, perhaps oddly, several quarries, including those at Linton and Bradnor Hill. They also include delightfully named sites, such as Hill Hole Dingle, the River Lugg Meanders and Bushy Hazels.

GARDENS

In addition to Long Meadow near Ivington, home to *Gardeners' World* expert Monty Don (not open to the public), incalculable gardens fill the county with inspiration and scent. Sized from the smallest to hundreds of acres, only five are designated RPGs (Registered Parks and Gardens) on the NHLE:

Holme Lacy	Whitfield, St Devereux
Kentchurch Court	Hill Court, Walford
Moccas Court, Staunton-on-Wye	

(Source: NHLE)

The following are but two gardens open to the public (at time of writing):

The Laskett Gardens, Much Dewchurch – when taken together, they form 'one of the largest private formal gardens to be created in England since 1945'. Sir Roy Strong, historian, broadcaster and landscape designer, together with his late wife, Dr Julia Trevelyan Oman, created a series of 'rooms' that narrates the history of their marriage and the power of the muse. Water features, statues and parterres join avenues, knot garden, topiary, and even a prairie-style border. (Source: www.thelaskettgardens.co.uk)

Stockton Bury Gardens, Kimbolton – set within a working estate, these gardens border a neighbouring orchard, remains of medieval fishponds (more a lake!) and an array of historic buildings that include the Cider House, dovecote and parochial Tithe Barn (now a restaurant). The gardens themselves were established toward the end of the nineteenth century, though evidence of much earlier occupation is never too far. Intervening years of neglect, when nature reclaimed much of its own, led to the gardens' re-discovery and its restoration as a labour of love. From the era of Victorian leisure and good, honest work, the gardens today bear evocative names, gravel walks languidly fusing the present with the past. (Source: The Stockton Bury Gardens guide)

TREES

As well as its orchards, the county has long been famed for its bountiful trees. Its oaks, for example – still seen in vast linear forests at Rushen Wood and elsewhere – were once so innumerable they were unflatteringly known as the 'Herefordshire weeds'!

Great tracts of woodland and dense forest greeted (and pre-dated) William Cobbett's nineteenth-century 'ride' from Gloucester to Ross: 'the finest I ever saw … of all kinds surpassing upon an average any that I have before seen in England' (Cobbett 1830). He also noted how 'very fine' the trees were, especially along the route to Hereford from Bollitree Castle.

'In 1805,' Clarke wrote a century later, 'a man standing on an eminence near Mordiford and looking eastward would see woodland stretching as far as the eye could reach … ' (in VCH 1908).

Nothing now remains of **De La Haye** (Haywood), the royal forest 'which at one time extended nearly to the city [Hereford] Gates and ranged for miles over the districts to the south and south-west' (Johnson 1882). Its timber was used in building Hereford Castle and in repairing the former Wye Bridge.

'Ancient' Trees

Particular specimens have long been revered, for their size, age and folkloric connections:

Great Oak, Hurstway Common, Eardisley – supposedly the last tree standing from a once mighty forest; measuring over 30ft about its trunk and said to be 1,000 years old.

St Dubricius, Whitchurch has a tulip tree three centuries old, which flowers every June through to July.

'Millennium' Yew, Munsley churchyard – claimed to be 'one of the biggest and oldest in Herefordshire'.

King Oak, Moccas Park – set within the present parkland (not open to the public), this vast, ruinous oak is said by some to be two millennia old (though such claims may come from the reputed age of Christ's birth, and its sign as God's majesty on Earth).

Gospel Oak (e.g. Ross-on-Wye) – oak trees (also sometimes elm or ash) where biblical texts were recited during Rogationtide and 'beating the bounds' (woe betide those who encroached on the 'parish'!). An authority no less than Charles Dickens claimed a Gospel Oak stood at Ross-on-Wye.

Great Oak Forest, Moccas – within which, according to Kilvert, the boars foraged on acorns and gave the place its name (from the Welsh *moch*, meaning swine).

Woodlands in Herefordshire
(as listed by the Forestry Commission)

Haugh Woods, Mordiford – entirely a SSSI
Queens Wood – straddles the Gloucestershire border
Bedstone Hill – to the north and shared with Shropshire
Hereford Woodlands – ten woods scattered around the county
Vinnalls – part of the Mortimer Forest where it extends into Shropshire off to the west
Wapley Hill – close to the Welsh border

WEATHER

It is quintessentially British to bemoan the weather, though dear old Cobbett attempted some hope:

> be this as it may, this summer has taught us, that our climate is the best for produce, after all; and that we cannot have Italian sun and English meat and cheese. We complain of the drip; but it is the drip that makes the beef and the mutton.

In 1697, a hailstorm of epic proportions rained terror on one part of the county. At Westhide (near Withington), 9in stones 'destroyed all the Poultrey, Garden Stuff, Corn, Grass, and most of the Fruit Trees in the Parish, but kill'd no Men nor Cattle, but hurt several, and broke most of the Windows'.

The Reverend Phillott, though, turned to biblical warnings during times of great flood, likening the one at Staunton-on-Wye on 5 February 1852 to the 'terrors' of the second coming of Christ. With no sense of shame, he urged his parishioners to see a God-given chance to take stock of the world, and of its miserable souls within.

In the winter of 1879–80, more than a quarter above the average rainfall produced the most disastrous floods throughout large parts of the county. A full fourth of its sheep were lost, either to drowning or unsavoury rot of the liver (caused by the flat worm, also called fluke).

4

BORDERLANDS

The Herefordshire border, in particular that shared with Wales, has been ceaselessly contested. At the heart of the troubles lay the several claimants: Romans, Saxons, Normans, the medieval Marcher Lords – and the perennial Welsh foe.

Fortification of the landscape and towns have left an historical mark, not least in:

- The nation's greatest concentration of castles
- Its lengthiest ditch
- And fiercest wars between men, women, princes and kings …

A VERY BRIEF SUMMARY

Under the Romans, the area served as a base for forays into the Welsh heartland, and their rich natural deposits – gold, silver and lead (see p.14).

Offa, King of all Mercia, built his great Saxon dyke that still carries his name (see below).

Not that borders sufficed. Sporadic assaults on Hereford – one of Alfred's great ninth-century *burhs*, established against Scandinavian threat – spilt rivers of blood and ravaged the town.

Into this cauldron came William, the conquering king, and through him his Lords Marcher, tasked with control – but left free to feather one's nest, as it were.

And beyond such a shambles, the running of the borderlands took an unusual form. *Stradel* (the present day Golden Valley) and *Archenfield* (Arcenfelde, *Ergyng*) lay betwixt and between. Neither English nor

Welsh, they became the *commotes* (*cwmwd*): administrative areas to the west of King Offa. Having Welsh culture, religion and aspects of trade, they fell outside the hundreds but were forever beholden to the new Norman lords – paying with *sestiers* of honey if not regular cash.

Amidst great death and rebellion, the medieval lords took gradual control – of one another, the Welsh and their lands. The real fear of conquest, in the thirteenth and fourteenth centuries at least, was neatly summed up by the lords' motivations for the borderland wars:

> the thirteenth and early fourteenth centuries [produced a] history of a group of great feudatories swayed by two powerful, but opposite, influences, which alternately obtained the ascendency – jealousy of … royal authority and desire for the support of the crown against the Welsh princes. (VCH 1908)

This long line of Welsh leaders was not so easily quelled and Hereford, more than anywhere else, suffered their wrath. Brutal oppression brought brutal affray. The city lost castles, cathedrals … the countryside even more.

Ownership of the land in the borders oscillated with fervour – great destitution where once had been hope. Vast swathes, once under the plough, had when Domesday was written become thicket and scrub. Little more than hostile *wasteland*, they bore little purpose other than *nobody's* land (better *they* don't possess it than ever *we* did).

SELECTED KEY DATES

1052   Gruffydd ap Llywelyn, King of Gwynedd, ravages Leominster.

1055   On 24 October the same Gruffydd, now Prince of All Wales, attacks Hereford. Two miles from the city, his ill-trained opponent makes the fatal mistake of fighting on horseback, a Norman routine. The city is sacked, its castle, cathedral and town all ruined or lost. Though the castle surrendered with little fight, the Welsh destroyed the cathedral. Seven canons were brutally slain at the West Door as they rashly resisted the mob.

1062   Harold Godwinson, Earl of Hereford since 1058, who fortified the town against further attack, takes to the sea to wreak his revenge.

The lives of the Welsh are only secured when they murder Gruffydd their leader. Harold takes his head to Edward the Confessor – self-proclaimed King of the Isles.

1066–9 William FitzOsbern, appointed first Norman Earl of Hereford, made frontier guard by William I. He refortifies Hereford Castle. Edric the Wild, a powerful *thegn* with lands in the county, allies himself to Llywelyn's successors, Rhiwallon and Bleddyn. The three ravage the county 'as far as the bridge over the River Lugg'. William I issues instructions to build *castella* along the border with Wales.

1070 The end of Edric the Wild. His lands and estates are sequestered and shared, his power withdrawn. (Though he later fought for the king during his battles in Scotland.)

1070 William FitzOsbern enlarges his kingdom, building his castle at Monmouth and making Radnorshire his.

1071 Feudal lords vie for power, with de Lacy and Mortimer the two most powerful kin.

1215 Border troubles anew – Giles de Braose, Bishop of Hereford, joins forces with Llywelyn ap Iorwerth ('the Great'). The pair take Shrewsbury.

1216 King John, under threat from the French, hides at Hereford Castle and pleads (vainly) for help from the Welsh.

1258 Llywelyn ap Gruffydd ('the Last'), grandson of Llywelyn the Great, becomes sole ruler of Wales ...

1262 ... and with Leicester (de Montfort), during the Baronial Wars, ravages Mortimer's Herefordshire (as far as Eardisley, Wigmore and Weobley) and imprisons the bishop.

1277 Edward I puts down Llywelyn ap Gruffydd's aggression

1282 Second Welsh uprising fails.

1284 Edward I's 'Treaty of Rhuddlan' brings an end to the wars

1400 Owain Glyndŵr, declared the last native Welsh prince, instigates a revolt against Henry IV. Wreaks havoc on Herefordshire castles and lands. Fights for twelve years before he mysteriously escapes and is said to have lived out his days with Sir John Scudamore of Kentchurch, who secretly married Alys, his daughter. Reputedly dies *c.* 1415–16, and is buried in secret – several locations are claimed as his grave. One of the strongest is near Monnington Court, on the edges of Vowchurch.

OFFA'S DYKE

Offa's Dyke is a late eighth-century earth bank and ditch, running from or near Prestatyn/Mold in the north, to Sedbury Cliff overlooking the Severn. The dyke is 149 miles (220km) long, of which at least 81 are constructed earthwork. Over 2m high and 18m wide (including ditch), it is the nation's largest linear earthwork.

Built by 'gangs' in discrete sections, the entire structure is credited to the Mercian King Offa, according to the writings of Asser of St David. The Herefordshire stretch continues to entice great debate. With only 6 miles 'known' in the county, many believe it never came here. Others though maintain it has simply been ploughed flat.

Local Names
Names for Offa's Dyke as it passes through the county:

Rough Moor	Riddox	Rowe Ditch
Grim's Ditch	The Ley	

Scheduled Monuments
Several sections in the county are scheduled monuments. The following show the NHLE listing number (and local HER). Please keep to public rights of way and/or the Offa's Dyke Path during visits:

- SM 1001737 (SMR 949): Offa's Dyke: the section extending 230yd (210m) N and S of the Old Barn near Kenmoor Coppice (SE of Bowmore Wood) (NGR SO 3950 4553)
- SM 1003776 (SMR 376): Offa's Dyke: the section extending 300yd (270m) crossing the railway W of Titley Junction (NGR SO 3242 5811)
- SM 1001731 (SMR 353): Offa's Dyke: Rushock Hill section, extending 1,630yd (1490m) E to Kennel Wood (NGR SO 3009 5960)
- SM 1001736 (SMR 948): Offa's Dyke: Upperton Farm, two sections extending 195yd (180m) and 370yd (340m) S from Yazor (NGR SO 3946 4680)
- SM 1001738 (SMR 950): Offa's Dyke: the section extending 950yd (870m) N and S of Big Oaks (NGR SO 4040 4379)
- SM 1001735 (SMR 5577): Offa's Dyke: section NW of Holme Marsh extending 615yd (560m) to the railway (NGR SO 3349 5501)
- SM 1005358 (SMR 8219): Offa's Dyke: section S of Riddings Brook on Herrock Hill (NGR SO 2764 5959)
- SM 1005525 (SMR 947): Offa's Dyke: the section N of Upperton Farm, extending 175yd (160m) (NGR SO 3943 4720)

- SM 1001732 (SMR 354): Offa's Dyke: the section extending 165yd (150m) N from Berry Wood (NGR SO 3239 5876)
- SM 1001733 (SMR 352): Offa's Dyke: the section 630yd (580m) long W of Lyonshall (NGR SO 3279 5599)
- SM 1001734 (SMR 351): Offa's Dyke: the section E of Garden Wood, extending SE 85yd (80m) (NGR SO 3313 5538)

(Sources: The NHLE, Historic England and Herefordshire's HER)

Offa's Dyke Through Herefordshire

The following brief summary is based on the Herefordshire VCH (Victoria County History), Herefordshire's HER (Historic Environment Record), Historic England's NHLE and on modern mapping (see bibliography). Please note: the Offa's Dyke Path National Trail (see p.86) does not always follow the line of the dyke. The information given here relates to the monument.

Owing to intense Welsh resistance, the line of the Dyke through Herefordshire is more altered and broken than anywhere else. Parts were rebuilt, along a different alignment, on at least one separate occasion. Its intermittent survival might owe as much to the degradable stone and marl used in its initial construction. Nonetheless, there is still plenty to see.

Offa's Dyke arrives into the county in the west at a point south of Knill Garraway Wood, near Knill. It runs east before turning sharp right, south as far as Holme Marsh, where it then peters out. This stretch is believed to be Offa's first attempt at building defences.

His second, more successful attempt emerges from Kennel Wood, runs eastwards to Scutchditch Wood, on to Green Lane, before arriving at Stocklow and heading off to the Pembridge Road. From here is the best-preserved part of the dyke:

strik[ing] south in a straight line across the Arrow valley, a mile in length, broken only by the river, to a point on the Kington Road half a mile from Pembridge. This bank presents all the features of the best-preserved parts of the Dike (sic) and is locally known as the 'Rowe Ditch'. (VCH)

Heading south through Yazor Wood, it emerges coherently at Claypits, before continuing to the west bank of the River Wye at Bridge Sollers (just below the modern A438). Now the River Wye, Herefordshire's main waterway appears to take over in lieu of the dyke. Only on the far (east) side of Hereford do its remains reappear.

In Bartonsham, at Rowe, or Rough, Ditch, it sets off farther east – along Vineyard Ridge, through Titley Court to the Mordiford Road, and on to the so-called Franchise boundary stone. The dyke's survival above ground now becomes quite sporadic but, having forded the river (Lugg), it becomes well defined once again – at least by Mordiford Cockshoot.

Eventually reaching Marcle Ridge, it turns south and runs into one of its most enduring stretches. After 1½ miles, above Woolhope Valley, it disappears beneath the town of Ross-on-Wye, crossing the Gloucestershire border, and is thought to head south as it follows the Wye.

CASTLES

With over 130 Herefordshire castles, the subject deserves its very own book! Listed here, then, are just a few of the favourites ...

Pre-Conquest (Norman) Castles

Such were the troubles in this borderland county that Norman lords were sent to maintain order long before 1066. Indeed, Herefordshire has three of only four pre-conquest castles known throughout England:

Richard's Castle – Founded in 1052 by Richard, son of Scrope (Scrob), a Norman favourite of Edward the Confessor. Positioned in the north, it monitored edgy Welsh feeling. By 1200, the Mortimer family, one of the country's new powerful elite, had taken ownership of the castle, together with its markets and ex-common rights. However, the castle and surrounding areas soon suffered greatly, not just from its geographic position but family ill fortune as well. By the time of the Dissolution by Henry VIII, its importance had faded. Today it is marked only by the remaining earthworks, though there is the occasional ruin.

Hereford Castle – first built sometime before 1052 by Ralph, son of the Count of Vexin, who was made Earl of Hereford in 1046 (source: www. herefordshire.gov.uk), it stood on what is now known as Castle Green.

Re-built *c.* 1066 from the ruins of Gruffydd ap Llywelyn's attack some eleven years earlier. Earl William of Hereford duly erected a new defensive colossus. Its ramparts were so vast, and its defences in stone, it was later considered to be on the scale of Windsor! In 1869, it was described as possessing:

a semicircular wall defended with towers and strengthened with a wet moat (Leland's *ubi non defenditur flumine* (1711). The entrance was on the north-eastern side over a great bridge of stone arches with a drawbridge in the middle, and the eastern or outer bailey to which access was thus gained contained within it the chapel, the mill and the barracks and stabling. The smaller or inner ward had also a strong wall and deep moat and in it was situated the keep, built massively on a lofty artificial mound.

(Robinson, 1869)

A pivotal centre of political intrigue, it was successively held by King Stephen, Matilda and by both sides in two national wars – Roses and Civil.

In 1139, Geoffrey Talbot assaulted the castle, in revenge against Stephen's earlier attack (see p.177).

In 1262, during the baronial wars, Earl Mortimer defended the castle against the contrivances of Leicester and Llewellyn the Last.

In April/May 1265, Prince Edward (later Edward I), was held prisoner at Hereford Castle after his ignoble defeat to Simon de Montfort at the Battle of Lewes. While exercising his mount at Widemarsh, north of the city, he affected a daring escape. Tiring his guards and their horses with his continual racing, he leapt on to a fresh ride and bolted away, finding sanctuary with the Mortimers at Wigmore Castle.

With peace came Hereford Castle's eventual demise – a process begun with Edward's conquest of Wales (1277–82). Little but ramparts and a section of moat are visible today.

Ewyas Harold Castle – commonly accepted as the first castle in England, a fortress that commanded the Dore and the Welsh. Also known as Pentecost Castle – after its founder in *c.* 1050 – its more familiar name comes from Harold of Ewyas, the first resident lord. Under him, a priory was erected inside the bailey.

As times changed, and Norman lords faced expulsion, the castle became a last bastion of hope. It, too, fell soon after, being almost razed to the ground.

Re-built by Earl William FitzOsbern, it also succumbed to the borderland curse – this time, Owain Glyndŵr finishing the task. Charles I noted the existence of the ruins, but all traces were lost not long after.

Norman Castles

The proliferation of *castella* built in the borders accounts for the vast number of castles built around 1086 (Domesday). Here are but a few:

Brampton Bryan Castle – seat of the Harley family for over 700 years, it began life as one of de Mortimer's vast possessions. Built between the Conquest and Domesday, first the de Bramptons, then Harleys (through marriage) took temporary charge, leading indirectly to one of history's most famous stand-offs and the castle's ignominious end.

In the Civil War, the Harleys were a rare Parliamentarian family caught up in a Royalist shire. As a sitting MP, Sir Robert went off to London, leaving his wife – the delightfully named 'Lady of Letters', Brilliana – to hold out against the ongoing assault. For several months, she held firm, despite a crumbling castle and her own weakening health. When, in October 1643, she died from pneumonia, she became yet another 'silent' victim of civil unrest. With the castle now duly surrendered, Royalist hatred fanned the flames of their fires, destroying what was left of the pitiful shell.

Clifford Castle – one of the more evocative and romantic of Herefordshire castles, Clifford was established soon after the Conquest, to protect William's new lands from the Welsh in the west. Erected on land laid waste by those troublesome neighbours, the castle was built by William FitzOsbern on the orders of the king. Sound orders they were, for Clifford Castle lasted as long as the threat from the Welsh remained real, garrisoned throughout until Glyndŵr's revolt (fifteenth century).

Eastnor (Brosnil) Castle – another of the ruins Cromwell (actually it was the Royalists this time) 'knocked about a bit'. Constructed in the mid-fifteenth century, this crenellated castle appears to have been more a statement of pride than a defender of men. Though possessing the main attributes of a castle, its opulence and splendour betrayed its true purpose.

Built by Richard Beauchamp, son of the Lord Treasurer to Henry VI, it attracted attention for all the wrong reasons when, in 1644, it succumbed to Parliamentarian attack and a later Royalist charge.

Goodrich Castle – first constructed of timber and earth, this motte-and-bailey castle was constructed by Godric Mappestone (from whence comes its name). It was later replaced in stone as part of the Norman defences and from its vantage point overlooking the valley it was able to control the area between Monmouth and Ross-on-Wye.

Constructed from red and grey sandstone, the castle was relatively small, indicating its primary function as defence rather than luxurious home. Nevertheless, its facilities included an array of comfortable rooms: a *solarium* (private quarters), buttery, numerous *garderobe* (water closets) and a Great Hall with large windows overlooking the Wye.

Goodrich has always played a critical role in notable wars: The Anarchy wars, between Stephen and Matilda; the Wars of the Roses, when its occupiers, the Talbots, supported the Lancastrian cause; and the Civil War of the seventeenth century, during which Goodrich was the very last castle to hold out for the king. It finally fell, in 1646, to a night-time assault led by Parliamentarian Colonel John Birch (see p.73). Heavy shelling from his infamous cannon – re-named 'Roaring Meg' – undermined the foundations and led to surrender. It survives to this day, on display at the castle.

Since then, William Wordsworth described Goodrich as 'the noblest ruin in Herefordshire' (in Hull and Whitehorne 2008: p. 37). A burial ground, pre-dating the castle's main ditch, was discovered in 1988.

Weobley Castle – one of de Lacy's eleventh-century piles. The second castle on this site even now boasts unmistakable earthworks. From such a bold impression, however, came the wrong kind of attention …

In The Anarchy wars, Stephen wreaked havoc on Matilda's supporters, especially Geoffrey Talbot who set out from Weobley Castle to burn Hereford south of the Wye (see p.176). The vengeful Stephen besieged the castle in 1140.

A new incarnation was constructed by Walter de Lacy *c.* 1213, and from here the varying fortunes of history and war were once again observed and engaged. In 1535, Leland the antiquarian recorded 'a goodly and fine building, but somewhat in decay'. And in the early 1800s, Cooke noted 'the site is now converted into a bowling-green'!

Wigmore Castle – one of those piles that owe more to their reputation than actual physical grandeur. This modestly sized castle was the seat of de Mortimer (see also Brampton Bryan) where he controlled all his lands – on both sides of the border.

It was built in *c.* 1067, under William FitzOsbern, as a border post on the wasteland of Merestun. In 1075, he forfeited his lands after a failed rebellion against William the Conqueror, and Ralph de Mortimer was granted the spoils.

Its renown for firing up rebels was forever entrenched when Hugh de Mortimer, Ralph's son, stood firm against Henry I, so that the castle was seized until Stephen's ascent.

Its strategic importance was once again recognised when Henry II spared its destruction when putting down rebellious lords in 1155.

The Mortimer line would rebel once again, when Roger, 1st Earl of March sided with Queen Isabella and led the assault on Edward II (see p.178). Through the boy-king, Edward III, he effectively ruled all England until Edward became a man, and had Roger hanged at Tyburn as a treacherous foe.

The Mortimer name, through marriage and war, has played several aces in the history of England. After the castle had passed through the hands of numerous successors, Lady Brilliana of Brampton Bryan (see above) secured Wigmore Castle, only to demand its total destruction when preventing Royalist attacks.

'Illicit' Castles

Unlicensed castles (*castra adulterina*) – thrown up without a license to crenellate – appeared across England during The Anarchy wars. Downton and Bredwardine in Herefordshire were claimed as examples.

A Chain of Command

On its border with Wales, a string of 'lesser' castles was established by paranoid lords. Their importance was proved when Henry IV (r. 1399–1413) ordered their re-fortification in the face of Glyndŵr's men. The many examples included:

Dorstone Castle – though its origins are uncertain, the fleeing Charles I found safety there as he made for Holme Lacy in 1645.

Snodhill Castle – guarded the northern entrance to the Golden Valley (*Stradel*), on land probably held by the famed Hugh the Ass. Built *c*. 1127 by Robert de Chandos, over the years it withstood unfriendly attention from both the Welsh and the Scots: succumbing in the seventeenth century under an assault by Earl Leven (see p.24).

Urishay Castle – more of a fortified manor than a castle: its castellations were for means of defence as much as the need to impress.

Some Fancifully Named Castles

Comfort Castle near Leominster
Mouse Castle in Cusop
Wheelbarrow Castle at Stoke Prior

(Further reading: 'Gazetteer of Herefordshire Castles', *Herefordshire Through Time* (see bibliography))

MARCHER LORDS

The history of these powerful nobles can be traced back to the Conquest when William I appointed his first earls of Chester, Shrewsbury and Hereford – the latter being William FitzOsbern, who responded to his task with the building of castles, often on land laid waste by the ravages of war.

The first Marcher Lords proper came from four powerful families: Mortimer, Bohun, Marshall and Clare.

In the face of renewed Welsh unity under Llywelyn ab Iorwerth (Llywelyn the Great), these self-styled rulers adopted castles, battles and their long history of gain.

As well as sitting in Parliament – but beyond state control – they honoured the king in irregular ways, such as providing four silver spears to support the canopy at the royal coronation (as for Eleanor, Queen to Henry III) (Bradley 1906: p. 80).

First Lord Presidents of the Marches

In the aftermath of Edward I's conquest of Wales, and its separation into English-style counties, the Marcher Lords felt compelled to assert their rights in outlandish ways. The Crown forced upon them a new administration as well as the appointment of a Lord President of the Marches:

1469   John Carpenter, Bishop of Worcester
1482   Edward, Prince of Wales
1502   William Smith, Bishop of Lincoln
1513   Geoffrey Blythe, Bishop of Litchfield and Coventry
1525   John Vesey, Bishop of Exeter
1535   Rowland Lee, Bishop of Litchfield and Coventry
1543   Richard Sampson, Bishop of Chester
1549   John Dudley, Earl of Warwick
1551   Sir William Herbert, Knight of the Garter
1553   Nicholas Heath, Archbishop of York and Chancellor of England/ Thomas Young, Archbishop of York
1555   Sir William Herbert, re-appointed
1556   Gilbert Bourne, Bishop of Bath and Wells

(Source: Duncumb 1804 (*sic*))

During the fifteenth-century troubles, several treacherous Marcher Lords joined Glyndŵr in his spat with King Henry IV.

Such were the antics of the old Marcher Lords that Henry VII ordered their cessation – establishing instead the Council of Wales and the Marches. Formally constituted in 1502, the council was enacted by his son, Henry VIII. It too grew so corrupt that within three decades it was itself reordered and censured.

5

PEOPLE

Scores have lived, died, served or fought throughout Herefordshire's history. From royal mistresses to naturalists, composers to artists, those born, lived, died, even just visited have been celebrated for their social, cultural, even technological triumphs. Many born here have gone on to great things, while a wealth of famous graves record *in memoriam* those revered with pride. (Information comes from a variety of sources, including the *Oxford Dictionary of National Biography* (*ODNB*))

PROMINENT PEOPLE

Hatches, matches and mentioned in dispatches – an eclectic selection of (some) Herefordshire 'worthies':

Sir Richard 'Dick' Whittington (*c*. 1354–1423) – Lord Mayor of London, famed for his rags-to-riches escapades and that infernal cat! The real-life Sir Richard, popularly thought of as a Gloucestershire merchant, was 'probably' born at Sollers Hope.

(Robert) Francis Kilvert (1840–1879) – clergyman and diarist. Born to a country rector, near Chippenham in Wiltshire, Kilvert followed in his father's steps by becoming a curate and vicar on the border with Wales. His short life tragically ended whilst he was incumbent of the then newly restored St Andrew's, Bredwardine, as well as rector of nearby Brobury.

His repute as a diarist captured popular thought, especially as so much was written whilst he was a Herefordshire resident. Much too was lost to the ravages of time, and a bit to wanton destruction. Amongst the surviving entries are descriptions of nineteenth-century life, already fading in front of his eyes. He also made observations about the opposite sex, to modern eyes often inadvertently frank.

His headstone portentously reads, 'He being dead yet speaketh', a plausible hope that a man's writing may be read long after his death. So it has proved.

Kilvert officially died from peritonitis. Local gossip at the time, however, blamed pneumonia which he caught while awaiting a ride on the way home from his honeymoon. His pre-marital affair(s) and his death within a month of marriage may explain why in death, as in life, he rests apart from his wife; each occupy quite separate plots in Bredwardine churchyard.

Skeffington Hume Dodgson (*c.* 1836–1919) – vicar (continuing the clerical theme). The Reverend Dodgson, a firm favourite at St Bartholomew's, Vowchurch (1895–1910), was known just as much for his illustrious kin. One certain Charles Lutwidge Dodgson (the author Lewis Carroll) was none other than the minister's brother! Though Charles may never have come to the village, his connection was maintained through his consummate words, letters and other memorabilia on show in the church, which form the 'Skeffington Shrine'.

Rowland Vaughan (1559–1629) – gentleman farmer and founder of modern irrigation. Of no known relation to the present author (!), Vaughan was a 'lost soul' turned pioneer. He was said to have discovered his idea for improving the productivity of land while observing a molehill standing out in the rain. Where the animal had been, the water ran freely, causing vegetation to grow. The remainder was arid and barren. His theory of 'drowning the lands' had thus taken shape. However, in keeping with his mocked reputation, he at first courted great derision – until his revelation saw output on his estate soar from £40 to £300 every year. In hindsight, his improvement to farming cannot be overstated.

Eleanor 'Nell' Gwyn (ne) (1650–1687) – actress and royal mistress. Though the birthplace of Britain's most infamous courtier is often contested, lasting opinion favours a dwelling in Hereford, along Pipe Well Lane (since renamed Gwynne Street). Born into a family of clerics (and brewers!), she left for Covent Garden in London, along with her mother; where, it is said, she served drinks in a brothel and learnt the ways of the flesh. She later fell into acting, somewhat by chance, selling oranges at the Theatre Royal, Drury Lane. And, in a life of vivacity, soon attracted the attention of Samuel Pepys (who would eventually dub her 'pretty, witty Nell'). Subsequently, as King Charles II's

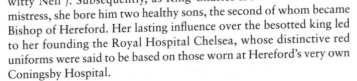

mistress, she bore him two healthy sons, the second of whom became Bishop of Hereford. Her lasting influence over the besotted king led to her founding the Royal Hospital Chelsea, whose distinctive red uniforms were said to be based on those worn at Hereford's very own Coningsby Hospital.

Lionel Thomas Caswall Rolt (1910–1974) – writer and founder of the Inland Waterways Association (IWA). Though born in Chester, 'Tom' Rolt lived for many years in Cusop, his father having based himself in nearby Hay-on-Wye. Rolt's obsession with canals started well before the Second World War, purchasing his uncle's horse-drawn 'flyboat', *Cressy*, and converting it into an early live-a-board vessel. In 1944, the (delayed) publication of his manuscript, *Narrowboat* (formerly entitled *Painted Boat*), cemented his place in canals folklore and myth. Rolt, though, had fallen in love with a dying way of life – facing not just decay but total extinction. Thus, in 1946, he and two friends set up the IWA, their mission to protect and preserve what they cherished the most. By the time of his own premature death, his contribution to the future of England's canals was already secured.

Alfred Watkins (1855–1935) – antiquarian and 'founder' of ley-line theory. A Herefordian throughout, he courted admiration and controversy in some equal measure. His contribution to landscape archaeology is hard to ignore, but his obsession with ley-lines and an accompanying theory of their impact on British prehistory has never truly been liked. His other passion, photography, brought him less equivocal fame, not least for his invention, the 'bee meter', which measured exposure and developing time: at least one accompanied Herbert Ponting, official photographer on Scott's ill-fated trek to the South Pole.

Elizabeth Barrett Browning (1806–1861) – campaigner and poet. Her formative years were spent at Hope End, the Georgian family estate near Ledbury, where she was educated at home. A sickly woman from the age of 15, she is believed to have developed an addiction to laudanum, an analgesic long before its revelation as a hallucinogenic drug. As an adult, she was introduced to major literary figures – including the Wordsworths, who visited the family at Whitney-on-Wye – and it is for her sonnet, 'How Do I Love Thee', that she will forever be known. Her impact on British social life, however, went far beyond her skills as a poet. An ardent campaigner for the abolition of slavery and improved conditions for children in work, her county connections live on in the Barrett Browning Memorial Institute and Clock Tower, erected in 1896 (but which Pevsner decried as 'really terrible').

John Kyrle (1637–1724), aka 'The Man of Ross' – immortalised in Pope's third *Moral Epistle*. The great landscape designer, businessman and philanthropist left a legacy of compassion, wealth and no small opportunity to the Herefordshire town. A descendant of an old county family, he was known to have acted as peacemaker, legate, effective lord and considerable 'worthy', leaving £40 to the Bluecoat School and his 'picturesque' landscape – The Prospect – which placed Ross at the centre of the seventeenth-century tour. He assisted the poor, in particular by ensuring apprenticeships, decent burials, life after debt and help for the sick. His memorial in Ross church, erected fifty-two years after his death, stood testament to his unending respect, while the 'desecration' of his Prospect gardens, by the then owner of The Royal Hotel, led to civil unrest in his memory. The site was subsequently given in perpetuity to the townspeople of Ross: a town that cherishes Kyrle as one of their own.

Henry Graves Bull MD (1818–1885) – naturalist and inspiration behind the extraordinary 'catalogue' of apples and pears, *Herefordshire Pomona*. Bull was a founding member of the Woolhope Naturalists' Field Club, still going strong after a century and a half. A keen mycologist (student of fungi), he helped make the club a precursor to the British Mycological Society. As a doctor, he found a link between social conditions and fatal diseases, including smallpox, typhus and scarlet fever. He observed contaminated water as a cause of the cholera outbreaks. His house overlooking Cathedral Close bears a heritage plaque, and his life and work are recorded on a memorial tablet in Hereford Cathedral.

Fair Rosamund (*c.* 1140–1175/6) – doyenne of royal hearts. She was born the daughter of a jumped-up steward who inherited Clifford Castle and

with it the name. King Henry II – who's wife, Queen Eleanor, was confined in her labours with the future King John – sought 'companionship' and 'succour'. By chance, he stayed the night at Clifford by Fair Rosamund's side. Now in a position of unquestionable power, she remained Henry's 'rose' for more than ten years. But then tragedy struck, as Rosamund fell ill in *c.* 1176 and retreated to Godstow's convent in Oxford, where she died shortly after. Claims she had been poisoned on Queen Eleanor's orders were mere conjecture, but the rumours and hearsay have never died down.

During the reburial of her bones, following an episcopal spat over her shrine-like, faux-royal tomb, the 'Rose of the World' gained her name from the epitaph on her new 'commoner's' grave:

> This tomb doth here enclose the world's most beauteous Rose,
> Rose passing sweet erewhile, now nought but odour vile.

(Speed, 1611)

A FOREST OF BLUE (GREEN OR GREY) PLAQUES

Instantly recognisable heritage plaques have adorned walls and railings for nearly a century and a half, commemorating Herefordshire people and their illustrious achievements.

'Herefordians' in Blue, Grey and Green

David Garrick (1717–1779), actor, theatre manager and playwright. Born at The Angel Inn (since demolished), Widemarsh Street, Hereford (see p.111).

Alfred Watkins (1855–1935), pioneer photographer and ley-line theorist – Harley Close, Hereford (see above).

David Cox (1783–1859), English landscape painter of the Birmingham School and early herald of the Impressionist movement. Taught at Hereford Grammar School and at a girls' school housed in the Gate House, Widemarsh Street. Lived in several properties around the county, including at Lower Lyde, All Saints, Parry's Lane and at Venns Lane, in Hereford.

Sir Edward Elgar (1857–1934), composer of 'Pomp and Circumstance', and 'Enigma Variations', forever associated with *The Last Night at the Proms*. Lived from 1904–1911 at Plas Gwyn, Hampton Park Road, Hereford (see p.109).

William Brewster (1665–1715), man of books, his due from Hereford – indeed the world – came from his generous bequest to All Saints church of his medieval manuscripts and collection of works. Since 1995, these have been housed in Hereford Cathedral's famous Chained Library (see p.107); the collection includes tomes on theology, literature, travel and science. Brewster was buried in Hereford Cathedral, but lived at Mansion House, Widemarsh Street, Hereford.

Lord Horatio Nelson (1758–1805) – Viscount and colossus of British naval successes. One of eleven children of a Norfolk cleric, his mother died when he was just 9. Aged 12, he accompanied his uncle, Captain Maurice Suckling, en route to the Falklands to put down a crisis and, although he never saw action, seldom looked back. Successes at Corsica, Naples, Copenhagen and on the Nile are considered some of his best. Larger than life, his death at Trafalgar was met with a national mourning the authorities had failed to predict. Nelson's connections to Herefordshire are as follows:

1. He stayed at the old City Arms Hotel, Hereford on 23 August 1802. The building stands on the site of the Saxon north gate; formerly the town house of the Duke of Norfolk, it is now Barclays Bank, Broad Street.
2. 'He visited Ross-on-Wye in 1802 and walked through these gardens' – Merton House Hotel, Edde Cross Street, Ross-on-Wye (Ross Civic Society & Mayor's Project).

In 1809, the people of Hereford erected a 60ft-high monument on Castle Green in the city, commemorating their hero and his naval commands.

Isambard Kingdom Brunel (1806–1859), gargantuan of Victorian civil engineering (and star of the London 2012 Olympic Games Opening Ceremony), erected Hereford Barrs Court in 1856, to the design of John Penson, architect – Hereford Railway Station.

John Scarlett Davis (1804–1845), artist admired for his landscapes, portraits and, more famously, his interiors of art galleries and churches – amongst them, the Louvre and Uffizi in Florence. Born 1 September 1804, he became a stalwart of his generation. A possible pupil of David Cox, he died tragically young from tuberculosis, which he may well have contracted on a tour of the Continent. Born at 2 High Street, Leominster.

'Nell' Gwynne (1650–1687), actress and royal mistress, purveyor of fruit. Allegedly born at a house (demolished in 1858) in – Gwynne Street (formerly Pipe Well Lane), Hereford (see above).

Rutland Boughton (1878–1960), twentieth-century composer of opera and choral music, and father of the first Glastonbury Festivals – Beavans Hill, Aston Ingham.

John 'Jack' Sharp (1878–1938), represented England at both football and cricket. Born at Eign Gate, Hereford (see p.79).

James Cowles Prichard (1786–1848) – so-called alienist, Victorian medic in affairs of the mind. Definer of 'moral insanity', in which the sufferer maintained a sense of decency in life, except on occasions when they suffered a moral decay over which they had little control. His contribution to the insanity debates, and on the handling of criminal lunatics, was renowned. Born at Millbrook House, Brookend Street, Ross-on-Wye (now a private residence).

Sarah Siddons, Actress (1755–1831) – daughter of local-born celebrity, actor and touring theatre manager Roger Kemble, sister to John Phillip Kemble, actor, she gained reputation for playing Shakespearian leads. An unusual square plaque commemorates where the patriarch lived – Church Street, Hereford (see also p.111).

HEREFORDSHIRE ARTISTS

As well as Cox and Scarlett Davis above, the county boasts an impressive list of artists, sculptors and potters who all found their muse in Herefordshire's charm:

Thomas Banks (1735–1805), sculptor – educated at Ross-on-Wye: winner of the Royal Academy gold medal for *The Rape of Proserpine*.

Dora de Houghton Carrington (1893–1932), painter – born March 1893 in Hereford, a breaker of convention ('a wild moorland pony') and subject of the film *Carrington*, starring Emma Thompson.

Penelope Butler née Carwardine (1729–*c*. 1801), miniatures painter – born at Withington, Herefordshire in 1729. She developed her skill with miniatures to earn money, but died penniless while provenance of her works remains hard to assess.

Frederick Michael 'Mick' Casson (1925–2003), potter – late of Upton Bishop, Herefordshire, overcame significant physical affliction to succeed with his individual style. Deviser and presenter of BBC's groundbreaking television programme, *The Craft of the Potter*.

David Cox junior (1809–1885), watercolourist – educated at Hereford Grammar School and, with his illustrious father (see above), became inked into Herefordshire's past. His acceptance into the Royal Academy came through his painting, 'Cottage in Herefordshire', in 1827.

Joshua Cristall (1767–1847), watercolourist – escaped London to purchase Granton Cottage, Goodrich, after which his best work reflected the inspiring Wye Valley. Established the county's first art exhibition, in Ross-on-Wye, but returned to London following the death of his wife. Though he died in the capital, he was buried at St Giles, Goodrich. Former President of the Old Watercolour Society.

Brian Hatton (1887–1916), artist – the 'young painter of genius' was born at Carlton Villas, Whitecross Road, Hereford, before moving aged 8 to Broomy Hill, Breinton. A natural artist, his rare talent led to success though he had not yet turned 9. His short life ended tragically in 1916, when serving with the British Army in North Africa. Surprised by a regiment of Turks, he was buried where he fell, but was later repatriated to the Kantara War Memorial Cemetery, Egypt.

MEN (AND WOMEN) OF LETTERS

John Edward Masefield (1878–1967), poet and novelist. Effectively 'orphaned' at a very young age (his mother died in childbirth, his father suffered years of depression before succumbing in hospital), this literary genius was born at The Knapp in Ledbury. He survived his guardians' dissuasion of his passion for books! A prolific literary output gradually earned him more than a string of tedious jobs, becoming a full-time writer at the start of the twentieth century. Declining a knighthood on more than one offering, he was Poet Laureate from 1930 to his death thirty-seven years later. His ashes were interred at Poets' Corner, Westminster Abbey: high reward that no doubt jarred with his desire to reach out to the 'common[er]'.

(Humphrey) Frank Owen (1905–1979), newspaper editor. Born in Widemarsh Street, Hereford, the son of the landlord at the old Black Swan pub. Elected Liberal MP for the city in 1929. An apparent strong drinker, he showed his unswerving nous as the editor of the old *Evening Standard* when, on war being declared, he made much of Hitler's vile reputation in order to boost circulation. Never one to avoid quarrels, he was a political activist right to the end. His contribution to London life earned him his freedom of that city.

Constance Dorothy Evelyn Peel née Bayliff (1868–1934), journalist and writer from Ganarew. The one-time managing director of Beeton & Co. found relative fortune and fame writing first as a single woman and subsequently as Mrs C.S. Peel. Her unconventional place in a masculine world focussed on the more archaic feminine world of 'running the home'. A prolific writer of books (including on cookery and home management), she died in London aged just 66.

Theophilus Swift (1746–1815), writer and close relative of Jonathan (*Gulliver's Travels*), born 1746 at Goodrich Castle. Oxbridge-educated and called to the bar in 1774, he fell foul of the law for alleged libel and spent twelve months in Marshalsea Prison. A firebrand through words, he published his *Vindication of Renwick Williams, commonly called the Monster*, proclaiming the innocence of that man imprisoned for violent assaults on women in London. He suffered a gunshot wound during a duel near the Uxbridge Road, London, following his opponent's outrage at his earlier attempts to slander the future Duke of Richmond!

Margaret Sibthorp née **Shurmer** (c. 1835–1916), editor. Of uncertain origins, though 'probably [born] in Hereford', she was an early exponent of women's rights. Editing the journal *Shafts*, she was quoted as saying it was her 'manifestation of my deep desire to serve the cause of women' (see *ODNB*). A fierce campaigner on many modern-day causes – from vegetarianism to sex education for all – she rose to prominence fighting for women to be able to 'choose': both motherhood and the practice of sex. Her fight for equality reached her editorial style, ardently removing any gender-specific pronouns used when making a universal point (e.g. chairperson).

Arnold Henry White (1848–1925), journalist. As a writer and political agitator, his failed attempts to become elected as first Liberal, then Liberal Unionist Member of Parliament, led to censure of a far higher kind. In 1907, advocating the immediate destruction of the new German High Fleet, the Kaiser demanded his removal from a party of visiting English writers if the trip were to proceed. Not content with the warning of a Teutonic threat, he wrote candidly about Irish Home Rule and national conscription. For a man born at All Saints in Hereford, he propelled himself onto the pre-war world stage with consummate ease. His most notorious moment at home, writing a piece for the then equally anti-German *Sun* newspaper, was considered sub judice, leading to his being imprisoned for contempt of court.

GONE BUT NOT FORGOTTEN

Herefordshire has many notable burials, some adorned with elaborate tombs, others with humble inscriptions.

Owen Tudor (d. 1461) – defeated Lancastrian and founder of the Tudor Dynasty – a casualty of the Yorkist victory at Mortimer's Cross. He was the grandfather of Henry VII, hounded as far as Hereford where the Earl of March, the future Yorkist King Edward IV, had him arrested and executed without mercy. A proud man, Tudor refused to believe his end was nigh, even at the very last:

wenyng and trustyng all eway that he shulde not be hedyd tylle he sawe the axe and the blocke, and whenn that he was in hys dobelet he trustyd on pardon and grace tylle the coler of hys redde vellvet dobbelet was ryppyd of.

Credulity of his impending doom came at last, as he mournfully proclaimed:

that hede shalle ly on the stocke that was wonte to ly on Quene Kateryns lappe, and put his herte and mynde holy unto God, and fulle mekely toke hys dethe.

His severed head was placed on the steps of the town's market cross, where, 'a madde woman kembyd his here and wysche a way the blode of hys face, and she gate candellys and sette aboute hym brennynge, moo then a C' (i.e. set 100 candles burning about his body).

His body was buried in the chapel of Greyfriars' church and a grey stone, set into the ground in High Street centuries later, sits near the site where his head was displayed.

Colonel John Birch (d. 1691) – Parliamentarian and Member of Parliament – has a grand, if not ostentatious, marble confection in Weobley parish church. Renowned for his political machinations as much as his night-time assault on Goodrich Castle – as well as the taking of Hereford against the king – the monumental inscription courts the same controversy he attracted in life.

After his son sanctioned the words (transcribed below), the authorities petitioned the Chancellor's Court to have the monument removed, seemingly with no great success. Royalist minds, in particular, objected to the apparent justification for the recent uprising against Charles I:

As the dignities he arrived at in the Field; and Esteem Universally yielded him in the SENAT-HOUSE [*sic*] Exceeded the Attainments of most; so they were but the Moderate and just Rewards of his Courage, Conduct Wisdom and Fidelity. None who knew him denyed him, ye Character of asserting & vindicating ye Laws & Liberties of this Country in War, and of promoting its Welfare and Prosperity in Peace; He was borne ye 7th of Sept 1626 And died a Member of ye Honourable House of Commons Being Burgess for Weobley May ye 10th 1691.

A modern note in the church gives his birth as 1616, though others have claimed an even earlier date.

Richard de la Bere, knight (d. 1514) – his entry here owes as much to his tomb as to his exploits in life. A work of art in brass, it remains in the south-east transept of Hereford Cathedral. Displayed in armour, standing and flanked by his two dutiful wives and their twenty-one children. Beneath the feet of his first, Anne, are a son and four daughters; by Elizabeth, to his left, six daughters and ten sons! Apparently a man of the family (!), he became surprisingly caught up in the forced marriage of one Margaret Kebell of Derbyshire to her unwanted paramour, de la Bere's own confidante, Roger Vernon.

In 1502, following a hasty (and illicit) wedding in Derby, the unwilling bride was brought to Herefordshire, to be secreted in de la Bere's manor house in nearby Clehonger. Following her unlikely escape, legal and drawn-out discussions aimed to bring de la Bere and the others to justice, but a king's pardon in 1509 put the matter to rest with no further reproof.

Meanwhile, his earlier involvement in Henry Stafford, Duke of Buckingham's revolt against King Richard III, saw him hide the luckless duke's son at Kinnersley Castle. The would-be usurper escaped over the border into the supposed safety of Wales, but his subsequent capture and execution in Salisbury spelt the end of the short-lived Buckingham Revolt of 1483.

General Sir Banastre 'Bloody' Tarleton (d. 1833) – commanding officer of the British Army in the US War of Independence – an unlikely occupant of Leintwardine parish church. A Liverpudlian by birth, he read law at Oxford before gambling away his late father's fortune, escaping only by purchasing a commission in the famed Dragoon Guards. As a soldier, he met with much greater success, becoming one of the men to capture General Lee. His reputation for unspeakable rigour in putting down American rebels was seemingly well founded. However, after his fortunes fell once again, he returned to England where he reignited a former affair, with Perdita Robinson, one-time mistress of the young Prince of Wales. Subsequently, and whilst still in the army, he became MP for his home city of Liverpool, defending the slavery trade which had brought such wealth to the port. His connection to Herefordshire was secured when he retired, dying and being inhumed in Leintwardine church.

Thomas 'Black' Vaughan (d. 1469) – though his infamy is left to a later chapter, Vaughan's tomb at St Mary's, Kington is worthy of mention here. It is a work of art in marble and alabaster, with ornate figures surrounding 'the Hergest beast' who died on the Banbury battlefield in 1469. Saints and angels accompany his effigy – and that of his wife, Ellen Gethin, 'the Terrible', daughter of Dafydd ap Cadwgan ap Phylip Dorddu (see p.97) – but it is either a piece of spectacular promotion or a terrible lie. His dark reputation for being unspeakably cruel has survived down the years. The dog lying faithfully at old Thomas' feet is both allegorical and – if myths are to be believed – an omen of fear.

Hamlet, Prince of Denmark (d. 362) – not the Bard's creation, but the subject of a Saxon monumental tablet declaring 'Hamlet the Jute. Died AD 362'. According to the fading inscription, set in the wall of Munsley's St Bartholomew's church, other pre-Christian burials accompany the Danish prince, appropriated no doubt by the local clergy to generate a 'third-sector' income – tourism! (Note: a yew tree in the churchyard is claimed to be the oldest and largest in the county.)

Robert Jones V.C. (d. 1898) – veteran of the 1879 Zulu War. Jones, at 21 years old, survived Rorke's Drift, being awarded the Victoria Cross for his heroic rescue of six comrades from the military hospital. Despite countless warriors literally beating the door, he engineered their escape while firing what little ammunition they had to keep the enemy at bay. When he later settled in Peterchurch, and though now married with five loving children, the horrors of that assault haunted him to his premature grave. A violent death from gunshot wounds to the head led to scurrilous rumours that he had taken his life. According to some, his grave in St Peter's churchyard lies 'the wrong way' – his body faces west (not east, as Christian tradition dictates) and his headstone is actually his footstone. Whatever the truth, the people of Peterchurch are proud to have a VC recipient buried nearby, forever more one of their own.

AND FINALLY ... A FEW HUMBLER PERSONS OF NOTE

Tucked away in what is now the Cafe Mundi at Hereford Cathedral, an inconspicuous tablet remembers an unnamed woman of considerable virtue:

> She was a woman of a most amiable disposition and exemplary character, mild and gentle in her manners, humble and modest

in her deportment, steady and sincere in her friendships, benevolent and charitable to the poor. She bore a long and painful illness with the greatest fortitude and patience and resigned her soul unto the hands of her Creator on 18 day of February 1797 in the 55 year of her age, leaving a sorrowing husband to lament her loss, and an only daughter to imitate her virtues.

Ledbury was evidently the place for long living, if **James Bailey**'s inscription is true (St Michael and All Angels). Youngest of three brothers, between them they amassed three complete centuries, James himself living to eight months beyond his 100th birthday. No mean feat in 1674!

A macabre work of sculpture (eighteenth century), in St Mary the Virgin church at Hope-under-Dinmore, depicts the Earl and Countess Coningsby (of nearby Hampton Court Castle) and their unfortunate child. The 2-year-old infant choked to death on a cherry, which the figure in stone grasps tight in his small, child's hand.

One of the nineteenth-century compilers of *Hymns Ancient and Modern* was the **Reverend Sir Henry Williams Baker** (d. 1877). He was vicar of All Saints, Monkland near Leominster from 1852 to 1877. His memorial bears a verse from his anthem – 'The King of Love My Shepherd Is'.

6

LEISURE
(GAMES, SPORTS & PASTIMES)

In an age when sport is seemingly more popular than breathing and when many of us have less time to indulge the latter if not the former, Herefordshire has made its own contribution to that elusive paradise: leisure. Not just in sport, but in country pursuits, childhood games, 'down time' and (of course, in the county of orchards) drinking!

FOOTBALL

At the time of writing, **Hereford Football Club** has risen from the ashes. A new team is born, by the people, for the people. A long way from the billionaire lifestyles of football's mega-rich, the Bulls have at least a rare opportunity to reconnect not just with the game, but with the county (and further afield).

The passion for the club was first formed more than a century ago. What a time they had ...

HEREFORD UNITED FC

Formed in 1924 out of two local sides, St Martin's and Rotherwas, the new aptly named Hereford United played non-league football for well over half of its colourful life. But, in 1972, when promotion to the professional league was still done by election, the Bulls (or the Lilywhites, for the purists) rose into the old 4th Division for the very first time.

With the club's fortunes soaring, player and manager, **John Charles**, became a Hereford hero. Through his celebrity exploits as a former player with Leeds and Juventus (one of the first British players to sign for a side playing in Europe), finances improved and their entry into the Football League was no longer a dream. Hereford United were a professional side.

But nothing compared to 1976/7 when Colin Addison, their talisman manager, along with the top goal scorer in all divisions, Dixie McNeil, steered them into the old 2nd Division, champions of the 3rd the season before. And by October, they sat just six places from the top tier of English football.

Away from the league, their most famous result came in 1972, and that **FA Cup** third-round replay against Newcastle United. Amidst boisterous scenes, and while still an amateur team, they dumped the high-flying Magpies out of the cup (see 'Ronnie Radford', below). **Edgar Street**, still the club's only ground in its entire existence, was never the same ....

Since then, despite strenuous efforts from the likes of Graham Turner (who twice managed the club and for a time became its majority shareholder), they were never to achieve their 1970s coups. Facing financial collapse, they were wound up in 2014, facing a tax bill and a terminal writ.

The end? Never. Hereford United would not be consigned to the history books yet. On 8 August 2015, a new Hereford United FC played their first game back in organised football – one league and several divisions below the pinnacle they achieved in 1976.

With their passionate supporters now controlling the club, only time will show how successful they prove. As its new crest, designed by a fanatical father and sons, proudly states: 'Hereford FC. Forever United.' We wish them well.

Colours

Hereford United once played in all white. At the end of the Second World War, with no material available due to rations, the team made their shorts from old blackout curtains, no longer needed against enemy attack. They have retained their 'new' colours ever since.

Players

A host of famous footballers began life in Hereford, either through birth or via their early development in their time with the club. For a select few, it was both, and for one, a memorable goal:

John 'Jack' Sharp

Local lad turned England legend, Sharp graced the fields of both football *and* cricket. Signed as a youngster by Hereford Thistle, the outside right (a footballing position of a past generation!), moved first to Aston Villa then to Everton, both founder members of the professional league. His wing-play, coupled with an ability to score, turned him into a firm favourite at the Lancashire club – like him, born in 1878.

In 342 games for the Toffees, he scored 80 goals and, in 1906, won the FA Cup with (in modern parlance) 'an assist' in the seventy-seventh minute. As Pickford, a football historian, would write later: 'No player's brilliance on the field was more vividly impressed on the minds of the ... spectators than Jack Sharp's' (source: www.evertonfc.com).

His switch to Test cricket made him an international hero, adding to his two footballing caps with his three with the bat. He scored an Ashes Test century in 1909 and, while still playing for Everton, became a regular starter for the local side, Lancs.

In time, he became a director at Everton, a position he kept for a number of years. One of the first to recognise commerce in football, he opened sports shops in Liverpool that were eventually taken over by JJB Sports.

Sharp died in 1938, three weeks short of his sixtieth birthday. In more recent times, he was installed as one of the first ten Everton 'Millennium Giants'.

Note: Sport featured strongly in the Sharp household. Bertram, Jack's brother, played professional football for Villa, Everton and Southampton, before returning to Everton where he too sat on the board. Like his younger brother, he also played cricket, in his case for his local side, Herefordshire County.

Ronnie Radford

Ronnie Radford the hero; the David who brought down Goliath. Hereford United's best-loved son secured his status in national folklore when he unleashed his 20yd 'screamer' into the top right-hand corner of the Newcastle goal. In 1972, on a churned-up pitch that looked more like Glastonbury after a very wet summer, the part-time carpenter got the ball from under his feet and etched himself into the annals of history. Such was the giant-killing act over Newcastle United that to beat a stronger opponent is forever more known as 'Doing A Radford'.

The man from Yorkshire, who joined the Bulls in 1971, had not in fact won the tie. That honour went to Ricky George, who netted in extra time of the FA Cup replay, ensuring the Edgar Street club won the match and footballing hearts.

It was Radford, though, who took all the plaudits. His strike was the first ever FA Cup score voted Goal of the Season (on BBC's *Match of the Day*); and to this day, BBC commentator John Motson describes it as the time of his life.

Kevin Sheedy
Like Sharp all those years before, Sheedy went on to an illustrious career with Everton FC.

Born in Builth Wells, 'Sheeds' signed for the Bulls at the age of 16. And it was Liverpool, not Everton, who gave him his break. Four years later, he switched to the blue half of Merseyside and it was they who got the most from his classy left foot.

In three years (1984–87), he won two First Division titles, an FA Cup, European Cup Winners' Cup, including a League and Cup double. And he would almost certainly have won the prized European Cup if English clubs had not faced their five-year ban after 1985.

Though born in Wales, Sheedy played forty-six times for the Republic of Ireland, scoring their first ever goal in a World Cup finals (in Italia 90). He infamously courted controversy in 1989, when he appeared to give the 'V' sign to jeering Liverpool supporters after scoring Everton's goal against his old club.

International Caps

Down the years, the club has produced a long list of players who went on to grace the international stage (see below). One, Brian Evans, turned out for his country (Wales) while still a player with the club.

HORSE RACING

The Sport of Kings has no current home in the county. But it has had several incarnations and a number of venues over the years:

Hereford Racecourse opened in 1771, but it was heavily re-ordered in the twentieth century. Meets took place typically in August, and the plate was an extravagant 10 shillings! The course, laid out on Widemarsh Common, survived the Enclosures Act of 1774 as the land all around was reclaimed.

The last regular (thoroughbred) race happened in 2012. Since then, only Arabian Horse Racing and the North Herefordshire Hunt's Point-to-Point have been run. (Stopn press: National Hunt racing is to return in later 2016.)

A course on **Bromyard Downs** was constructed in 1815 and proved instantly popular. By the end of the century, it drew up to 7,000 race-goers, thrilled by the combination of hurdles and flat. Of the then seven pubs, quenching the thirst of nerve-shredded betters, only the Royal Oak now remains.

In **Kington**, too, the racecourse stood high on the slopes. On Bradnor Hill from 1770, from 1825 it lay over on Hergest Ridge. It finally closed *c.* 1880, though its earthwork remains are still to be seen.

Freddie Fox, flat racing champion in 1930, lived in Kingsland near Leominster. He twice won the Derby (1931, 1935) as well as three other classics.

HISTORIC SPORTS

Not all 'sports' are remembered fondly. But their place in Herefordshire's history remains an incontrovertible fact:

Baiting

The dangers of **bear-baiting** (not just for the bears) were real enough for the woman killed in her bed in 1570, after the bear escaped and entered her house near Hereford.

Bull-baiting took place at the Corn Market in Leominster in 1794, after which much cleaning up was deemed necessary ... while pubs such as the Bull Ring in Kingstone seem to reference the 'sport', perhaps held in a nearby field.

Badger-baiting ... well, you get the idea.

Cockfighting

Once encouraged by King James and the post-Reformation population, cockfighting was a regular sight in Herefordshire villages. Cockpits were thought to exist at Craswall (church), Aymestrey, Wormbridge and Brilley.

John Andrews, trainer of fighting cocks, was buried at Peterchurch in 1799. His inscription paints a picture of greater humanity than perhaps his profession suggests:

> Alas, poor Captain, winged by cruel death,
> He pecked in vain, o'ermatched, resigned his breath,
> Lov'd social mirth, none dare his word distrust,
> Sincere in friendship, and was truly just.

Bare-knuckle Fighting

Fownhope produced a 'hero' of bare-knuckle fighting: Tom Spring (real name Tom Winter – geddit!), born at Witchend in the Herefordshire village. He became English Heavyweight Champion from 1821 until his retirement in 1824. Known more for his technique and fast feet than the strength of his punch, he retained his unbeaten title largely because no one in England would oppose him! His exploits drew crowds of up to 30,000 and were immortalised in Arthur Conan Doyle's *The Lord of Falconbridge*.

MESSING ABOUT ON THE RIVER

Though the Wye and the Lugg lack many large vessels, kayaks, canoes and all manner of small boats stipple the routes. Such a popular need to mess about on the water has its roots in the past ....

In 1878, Kilvert captured the romance and pleasure of a summer's cruise down the Wye:

> George Phillott came up from Moccas in his punt and ... I went down with him ... to Moccas, a lovely voyage with glorious evening lights and shadows on the water, indescribably beautiful.
> (Plomer 1944: pp. 333–4)

Modern canoe and/or kayak centres nearby (at time of writing and not exhaustive) are as follows:

Ross-on-Wye   Monmouth (Monmouthshire)
Symonds Yat   Hay-on-Wye (Powys)
Coleford (Gloucestershire)

(Source: www.wyevalleyaonb.org.uk)

CRICKET

Also from Kilvert, in 1870 he recorded the greater draw of leather on willow beyond eternal salvation! A Confirmation class deserter was made to explain that, 'he had to [meet] the 9 o'clock train with a pony to meet his master returning from a cricket match near Hereford, the Wyeside Wanderers against Portway' (Plomer 1944: p. 51).

From its earliest origins until the mid-eighteenth century, cricket resembled nothing close to the modern-day game. A wicket was a hole in the ground, into which the bat must be placed before the fielder could do the same with the ball.

By 1830, Herefordshire had its first regular side, the ancient **Herefordshire County Cricket Club**. Early games were played on Widemarsh Common, while practice matches occasionally took place in the grounds of Hampton Court Castle, a redoubtable yet unlikely sporting venue (see Archery below). But so stuttering was the start to the organised game, a second club, **Hereford City**, took up the bat, in 1836–37.

Towards the end of the nineteenth century, the two sides effectively merged. So great was their national standing that **W.G. Grace** himself organised at least three Herefordshire matches – as well as writing about cricket in *The Hereford Times*. In 1890, he brought twelve of his best men from neighbouring Gloucestershire to play out a draw on the **Wyeside Ground** (albeit against *eighteen* locals!). To the Herefordians' delight, the bearded colossus of cricket's wicket soon fell … for a measly one run!

1st innings — DR. W. G. GRACE'S SIDE		2nd innings	
W.G. Grace, c J. H. Barratt, b May	1	b Davenport	48
C. J. Robinson, b May	0	b Kirk	0
J. Cranston, b Cobden	23	run out	4
O. G. Radcliffe, c Phillips, b Cobden	56	b Kirk	20
H. H. Francis, b Cobden	3		
O. L. Evans, c Evelyn, b Cobden	4	c Kirk, b May	7
C. Harding, c C. S. Barratt, b Cobden	2		
S. de Winton, b Giles	16	not out	6
T. Taylor, c Daniel, b Kirk	1	not out	23
Roberts, b Cobden	8		
J. H. Iles, not out	2		
J. A. Bush, c Phillips, b Giles	7		
Extras	1	Extras	13
Total	124	Total (for 5 wkts.)	121

The current **Herefordshire Cricket Club** was formed, likes its footballing cousins, in the aftermath of their forerunner's demise. Founded in 1992, they have now played (and won) the Minor Counties Championship, contested the knockout MCCA Cup, and competed in the Unicorns 20/20 Challenge. Their matches are played on grounds around the county, including Brockhampton, Colwall, Eastnor and the Old Luctonians ground, Kingsland.

Famous Herefordshire Cricketers (Since 1836)
England Test players born in Herefordshire:

Reg Perks
Peter Richardson

Dick Richardson
John 'Jack' Sharp (see also p.79)

Herefordshire players to wear England Whites:

Chris Woakes   Martin McCague   Neal Radford

ARCHERY

Long after the wars fought by medieval archers, passionate toxophilites resurrected the art. At the time of Elizabeth I, archery had become a notable pastime but, three centuries later, had all but died. The first **Herefordshire Bowmeeting** was held in the summer of 1826, congregating on the lawns of Hampton Court Castle. Still going today, the meet has been held at some of the county's greatest estates. The Hampton Court Company of Archers, who meet every month, maintains the sport's local attachments.

BOWLING

The oldest bowling green in the world lies hidden away in the heart of Hereford town centre. Thought to date from 1484, it is fronted, conveniently enough, by the Bowling Green Inn, which itself sits (more or less) behind All Saints church. The Green was played every year from May to the end of the summer, though nowadays starts a month sooner, i.e. April.

GAMES

At the start of the nineteenth century, **billiard tables** existed at Lane's Coffee House and the Black Swan on Bridge Street, both in Hereford.

Fives Courts (a squash-like ball game played with the hand – hence, 'bunch of fives') existed at the Nag's Head, Hereford as well as at the Old Gaol. Courts were also found in Herefordshire churchyards, with a red line painted on a wall between two convenient buttresses! Craswall and Canon Pyon are recorded examples.

Skittle alleys could be found at the Thatched Tavern and the Aylestone Hill Coffee House, Hereford.

Our old friend Kilvert mentions (1870s) three bygone games: **Battledore & Shuttlecock** (badminton) which was played inside when the weather was rough; **Blindman's Bluff** which, for younger readers, involved a blindfolded player attempting to 'tag' all the rest; and the delightfully named **Fox-a-Dandley**, an early form of hide-and-seek. The cleric had 'no idea the old game was still played by the present generation'.

He also recalled tales of 'games and sports … fights and merriments, that went on in old times upon Bredwardine Knap.'

'What kind of games?' he once asked a local.

'I wouldn't suggest that they were of any spiritual good,' came the reply (Plomer 1944: p. 344).

ANGLING

The rivers Wye, Lugg and Monnow (and numerous others) attract fishermen (and women), these days more for sport than for gathering food.

Freshwater fish were once so abundant that salmon fell to just one pence per pound. Species once ranged from eels to lamprey, pike to carp. In attempt to harness commerce from such healthy supplies, fisher men with their profusion of weirs and traps inevitably led to their own downfall. Far fewer fish populate the rivers today.

WALKING

Modern walks today extend for miles. In the days of more modest endeavours, **Castle Green**, Hereford was the 'principal walk of the town' and 'one of the most complete in the kingdom'. Paid for by subscription and kept up by the Templar's Society (today by Friends of Castle Green), it remains a tranquil oasis on the former site of Hereford Castle. Find it via a hidden narrow passage over the moat behind Castle Street.

The Wye Valley Walk
With something for everyone, this 136-mile planned route takes the walker through every conceivable landscape, from gorge to mountain, meadow to river. Stretching from the Welsh hills at Plynlimon, to its confluence with the Severn and the Bristol Channel, its features and landmarks are both breathtaking and innumerable. In Herefordshire, it extends north of Hay and Rhydspence, through Hereford, Mordiford and south to Ross-on-Wye, eventually leaving the county beyond Symonds Yat.

Offa's Dyke Path
Offa's Dyke may have given its name to this National Trail, but in truth the walk diverges from the Mercian king's dyke at several points along

its sizeable route. Nevertheless, it is a splendid means of charting the English–Welsh border, and many of its 177 miles fall within the county between Lower Harpton in the north to Hatterrall Hill on the Black Mountain ridge.

(Some) Others

The Herefordshire Trail links the Malverns in the east to the Black Mountains in the west, along the course of 150 miles of breathtaking views. Links the five market towns of Ledbury, Ross, Kington, Bromyard and Leominster.

The Three Choirs Way turns music into steps, connecting the three great cities inextricably linked in the choral calendar (see p.109). It encounters at least three Herefordshire rivers – the Wye, Teme and Lugg – and joins up with the Wye Valley Walk.

The Vaughan Way, a long-distance path that links the Mortimer Trail and Offa's Dyke Path, both at Kington, with the Wye Valley Walk at Bredwardine, north-east of Hay. With 'loop walks' sprouting off and arriving at some of the county's best secret locations, it derives its name from the local eminent family.

The Mortimer Trail runs for 30 miles through the old lands of the once powerful lords. At times a strenuous walk, the many valleys, commons, hillforts and sights along the way reward the hardy. The trail leaves Ludlow to the south, crossing quickly into the county, and ends at Kington across to the west.

Monnington Walk, a delightful stroll through the famous seventeenth-century, mile-long stretch of Scotch firs planted by the then owner of Monnington Court, Sir Thomas Tomkins, to celebrate his election as a Member of Parliament in 1641.

The Three Rivers Ride, part of the National Bridleway Network, entering Herefordshire at Wolferlow and passing into Wales at Hay-on-Wye.

DANCING

Hereford's **Dancing Assemblies** took place at the Assembly Room (later the City Arms Hotel). They were usually held just one day a month (always a Tuesday), from October to February, sometimes to March.

Extra days were held when the organisers felt racy! According to an account of 1806:

> the assemblies are conducted with great decorum, and attended by the best company. The office of Master of the Ceremonies is performed by a President, who is chosen for every succeeding night, out of those who frequent the assemblies. (Rees 1806: p. 54)

LIBATIONS

In the reign of Edward VI (1547–53), only licensed taverns could sell wine in the cities and towns – and Hereford was given but three. When Queen Mary, the ill-fated daughter of Henry VIII, replaced Edward, a certain Johanne and John Kerry petitioned HM for just such a license – having been overlooked in the past and forced to cease trade. The fortunate pair elicited the following fulsome response:

> Mary, by the grace of God, Queen of England, France, and Ireland, defender of the faith, to all men to whom these presents shall come, greeting. Whereas, by an Act of Parliament made in the Parliament held at Westminster the first day of March in the seventh year of the reign of our most dearest brother King Edward VI, it was amongst other things ordained and provided that no person whatsoever within this realm of England and Wales, after the feast of St. Michael the Archangel then next following, should keep any tavern, nor sell nor utter by retail any kind of wine, to be drunk or spent in his or their mansion-house or other place in their occupation, by any colour or means, in any city, borough, or town, but only such persons as should be thereto named, appointed, and assigned, according to the form and effect of the said act, upon pain of such forfeitures and penalties as in the same act is expressed and contained: Nevertheless, as my loving subjects John Kerry, citizen and burgess of Hereford, and Johanne his wife, have made their humble suit and petition unto us, that it might please us to license and permit them to occupy a tavern, and sell wines by retail, as they used to do before making of the said statute, for that they should be otherwise compelled to put away their apprentices, journeymen, and other their servants, and to break up their household, to their utter undoing, having fifteen children, and none other trade or living but only by retailing of wines, wherein they had been brought up the most part of their

lifetime. We, therefore, minding that our said subjects should
be relieved in these particulars, are pleased by these presents, of
our special grace to give license and liberty, and do grant for us,
our heirs, and successors, to John Kerry and Johanne his wife,
that they during their lives, and the longest liver of either of
them, shall and may keep a tavern, and sell by retail any kind
of wine, to be drunk or spent in their mansion-house, or other
place in their occupation, within the citie of Hereford, in such
manner as they might have done before the making of the
said statute, without any loss, pain, forfeiture, imprisonment,
or penalty, to be by them sustained for the same. And further,
our will and pleasure is that the said John Kerry and Johanne
his wife shall in future have and enjoy the full effect, benefit,
and advantage of this licence and grant from the first day of
May last past, without danger or imprisonment to them for the
same. In witness whereof we have caused these our letters to be
made patent. Witness ourself at Farnham, the 5th day of July,
the fifth year of the reign. Given under the seal.

(Johnson 1882: 133–34)

Famed Inns

Green Man Inn, Fownhope – fifteenth century, where the Roundhead
colonel, John Birch, reputedly stayed the night before taking Hereford
in December 1645, and whose castle he bought after King Charles'
defeat (VCH 1908: p. 396). Formerly called the Naked Boy (connected
either with salmon fishing or sweeping the chimney?!), it later became
the local court house (a trap door survives). Tom Spring (see Historic
Sports), for a while its landlord, is depicted in a mural there.

Tram Inn, Eardisley – once a haunt of the coalmen bringing 'black gold'
from Brecon, and the reputed destination for the Eardisley Stampede
(see p.94). Originally a seventeenth-century inn, it is constructed of
black-and-white timbers and brick infill. It claims to be the first pub in
Britain to serve local Dunkerton's Organic Cider on draft (see p.124).

Rhydspence Inn – hugging the Welsh border near Hay-on-Wye, is a rare
survivor of a drovers' tavern. Built in 1380, so-say to serve pilgrims
en route to Hereford Cathedral, it retains signs of the droving *shoeing
station* where the cattle were shod before continuing along England's
metalled roads.

The splendidly named **Axe and Cleaver Inn** at Much Birch conjures up
images of mayhem and horror. The truth, though, is probably rather

less grim. Its origins are equally vague – with a seventeenth-century date most readily favoured.

Bunch-of-Grapes Tavern, tucked away in Hereford's Church Street (Narrow Capuchin Lane), dates to the early 1600s. One of the city's oldest, it was here that an official of the town read out the weekly letter from London.

The historic **Live and Let Live** on Bringsty Common is a seventeenth-century gem. A cider house from the mid-1800s, it claims to be the only pub in the county sporting a thatched roof.

The sign at **The Bunch of Carrots** in Hampton Bishop has to be one of the few in the country to have a root veg in its name! It apparently takes its name from a small rock formation within the nearby river!

Bromyard still boasts several inns, three of which are housed in black-and-white timber. **The Inn, Falcon** and **King's Arms** are all situated on High Street or Broad Street. The **Hop Pole**, equally ancient, overlooks the delightful surprise of the town's Market Square.

7

MYTHS, SUPERSTITIONS AND LEGENDS

WITCHES, WARLOCKS AND SEERS

Mary Hodges, 'maid of old irons', bewitched cattle and livestock and was seen at night to cross fire irons in the hearth and offer up Devilish 'prayers' (recorded 1662):

> she is observed to take the andirons out of the chimney, and put them cross one another and then she falls down upon her knees and useth some prayers of witchcraft ... and ... she then makes water in a dish, and throws it upon the said andirons, and then takes her journey into her garden. This is her usual custom night after night, which doth occasion fear that she intends mischief against ... her neighbours. (*Herefordshire Through Time*)

At **Whitney Toll Bridge,** the tollhouse keeper bewitched the waggoner's horses if they avoided paying the fee.

A local saying at Weobley and environs: 'If thee bist a witch, the Devil take thee; if thee bain't a witch, the Almighty bless thee!' But then nearby **Weobley Marsh** apparently hosted dozens of witches (in the late 1800s):

> From the bottom of Weobley Marsh to the top of Mainbury ... there were *fifty* witches, and [one] had power to call them all out and make them dance. (Leather, 2001)

Jack of Kent, Kentchurch, according to legend, was a medieval Satanist who sold his soul to St Nick in return for a mischievous imp. Jack, real name unknown, struck a deal that at the moment of death – whether he be buried inside or outside the church – his soul was the Devil's. Before his devilish fate took him, Jack left instructions to be buried within a hole in the wall of the church – being neither inside nor out. His soul thus remained free of the master's demands!

Several characters were claimed to be Jack, though none has been proved beyond all reasonable doubt. What is certain, however, is the veracity of the story, real enough in the minds of the locals who for centuries now have kept alive his salutary yarn.

FOLKLORE

Much of what follows is informed by Leather, Duncumb and Havergal (see bibliography):

A charm for **toothache**, once thought to be caused by a troublesome worm, was found in the records of Crasswall (*sic*), as 'written on a small piece of paper and sealed with pitch' (1886):

Christ met with Peter and saide unto him Peter what is the matter with thee. Peter saide: lorde I am tormented with the paine in my tooth. [But the Lord replied:] the worme shall Die and Thou shalt live and thow that shalt have this in wrightin or in memory shall never have the Paine in the tooth. Therefore believe in the lorde youre God.

Madley is given as the birthplace of **St Dyfrig**, the man who reputedly crowned King Arthur in the fifth century.

A particular **crystal ball**, or *berill*, kept secure in a closet in Brampton Bryan Castle, was used to cure ills and for divination. Visions would typically include herbs or spells or, in the case of a group of incompetent rogues, the names of those who had thieved from a clothier in Pembridge.

A **bag of woodlice** tied around the neck would ease the cutting of infant teeth.

A **plate of flour** placed beneath a rosemary bush on Midsummer's Eve would the next morning reveal a lover's initials.

Tying a **noose** used to hang a criminal around one's own head cured a headache!

In the same vein as **throwing salt** over the left shoulder:
- Sisters must never pass soap from one to the other
- Fire irons gathered together on the side of the hearth augers a quarrel (see Mary Hodges above)
- Never burn three candles in the home
- Bring in a plate of salt and a bag of coal to a new house, always before the furniture.

CALENDAR CUSTOMS

Hereford's 'Jack in the Green'

It is custom in Hereford on May Day to carry a Jack-in-the-Green around High Town. On a similar tack, several carved images of the Green Man, or foliate heads, are found in Hereford Cathedral, Kilpeck, Leominster Priory and Abbey Dore – to name but a few. It was common practice apparently to incorporate this pagan symbol into Christian churches in deference to 'the old ways'.

May Day

According to custom, May Day was either the first day of the month or Oak Apple Day (29 May) – the birthday of Charles II and the day, in 1660, when the monarchy was restored. The king, of course, had avoided his enemy by hiding in the Boscobel oak.

1 May, with its familiar maypole and fertility dances, was wont to descend into riotous japes. Brooms, pails and decorated arches all featured strongly. Bowers and arches were a prominent token in the May Day festivities in Bromyard, Bosbury and Broomy Hill:

> On the first day of May, the juvenile part of both sexes rise early in the morning, and, walking to some neighbouring wood, supply themselves with green branches of trees. Returning home, the boughs are placed against the doors and houses, and are kept there during the remainder of the day. The birch tree, being early in vegetation, is invariably chosen in this county for the first of May (Duncumb 1804: p. 209).

Oak Apple Day

On pain of being pelted with eggs, many in the county wore an oak leaf in the lapel, and the old carters adorned their horses' headgear with the same.

A bough of oak was placed on the tower of Kingsland church.

Eardisley's 'Wild West' Stampede

May Day saw the Herefordshire village transformed for one day into the US Wild West. In the 1970s, having returned from his years spent living in Canada, a 'local' established a lil' piece of home in front of the local Tram Inn – or the *Mountie* as it became known! The inn has since been renamed the New Strand at Eardisley.

Fownhope Heart of Oak Society
The Fownhope Heart of Oak – a forerunner of the Victorian Friendly Societies – celebrates its historic existence with an annual fair. Every Oak Apple Day (once on Whitsuntide), an oak bough is cut from the woods and draped in red, white and blue. Society members then dress their sticks with flowers and leaves, carrying them away to the Green Man Inn (see p.89).

The May Morris
One of the most curious May Day customs took the form of a race – not of horses, but of 'lusty' men who rode their sticks with a carved head finial, popularly called the hobby horse.

In 1609, it attracted such infamy (and pleasure) that even that most noble of towns, Bath, lost their patrons to Hereford – not just to watch but to take part in the famed Morris Daunce:

> Lords went a-Maying, the womb of the spring being great with [the] child of pleasure, brought forth a number of Knights, Esquires, and Gallants from many parts of the land, to meet at a Horse-race near Hereford, in Herefordshire. The horses having run themselves well-nigh out of breath, wagers of great sums being won and lost ... Thereupon (whilest the mettle of his braines were hot and boyling) a braggard undertook to bring a Hobbie-horse to the race, that should out-runne all the Nags which were to come and to hold out in a longer race, then any would be there.
>
> (Paraphrased from Lord Ruthen 1816)

A sight to behold. But consider this: the combined ages of these gallant eighteen knights and esquires was not a year less than 1,837!

> And so they dressed, for a Morris of old; as tabor, fiddle and racing struck gold. The names and the colours were given in full (if only we had space to impart them all). (*Ibid*)

Burning the Bush
Burning the bush was a New Year's tradition witnessed by, amongst others, Francis Kilvert:

> After I had gone to bed [after seeing in the New Year], I saw from where I lay a bright blaze sprung up in the fields beyond the river and I knew at once that they were keeping up the old

custom of Burning the Bush…From the Knap, the hill above the [Bredwardine] village masked by two clumps of trees, the whole valley can be seen early on New Year's Morning alight with fires.

(Plomer 1944: pp. 321–2)

A possible explanation of this old practise comes via Leather (2001). A ball of hawthorn hangs in the house all year, mistletoe acting as its companion, the latter only ever brought in on New Year's Day. At the same time, the old ball is taken from the house and set alight, the flames used to scorch the sides of the new. In certain parts of the county, this is then 'varnished' with cider.

An expanded description sees the burning bush carried across twelve ridges of a newly ploughed field, imbuing fertility on the crops to come and capturing bad spirits from the old year into the fiery ball. It was a poor omen if the fire died out before the last ridge was reached. But, if all had gone well, the men of the village gathered round the fire and toasted the New Year in that Herefordshire way – 'Holloa to cider!'

At harvest each year, the county went **a-scottering**. Similar to burning the bush, four (sometimes six) bachelor lads from the village would set light to a bundle of straw and dance around the ricks in a figure of eight. The usual accompaniment of cider and song gave thanks for the harvest just reaped.

INFAMOUS HAUNTINGS

The oft-told tale of **Black Vaughan of Hergest Court** (see p.75) features a character so monstrous he could not possibly be the author's relation!

In short, Thomas Vaughan was so cruel that upon his premature death in 1469, it was said the terrified locals put him in a double-skinned tomb. Nevertheless, his ghost carried on where his self had left off.

It began with reports that his faithful old dog had carried off his dead master's head from the battlefield near Oxford where Thomas had died. Whether or not true, Vaughan's spirit returned, and so too that faithful black hound … a connection that would find its way into Conan Doyle's Baskerville Hall. To see it now meant certain death.

One of the spectral forms Vaughan was said to adopt was that of a black bull that charged at parishioners, or startled their horses while pulling the carts. On other occasions, he took hold of the reins before steering them over the edge of the ridge.

Something had to be done. One night, armed with bibles and candles, twelve terrified priests incanted the menace, the feeblest at first becoming the saviour of souls. As he read from the Good Book, Black Vaughan's ghost appeared and gave out a piercing howl. The stoical cleric drew the hideous spectre down into the snuffbox he had brought for the act. And, with the nerves he had left, threw it far in the pond once kept by the court.

All was said to be silent … Black Vaughan's power no more …

And yet, five centuries on, the story is still told and his ghostly behaviour is said to have started again.

POETIC JUSTICE

From the same family – indeed, Thomas' wife who was also his cousin – comes another true tale of horrific revenge. Handed down through the writings of a certain Welsh poet, Ellen Vaughan – forever more known as Ellen Gethin, or Ellen the Terrible – was never one to let bygones go by.

In the mid-fifteenth century, before she was married, she and her brother lived as orphans at the same family seat (the aforementioned Hergest Court). But David, some years her junior, was tragically killed, losing a duel with his cousin, Sion Hir (John the Tall), of the Vaughans of Talgarth.

Intent on revenge, the stoical Ellen donned a male disguise, and attended a 'shoot' at nearby Llandewi. Challenging the 'Master of the Field', who by no accident was her target of hate, she declined the man's invitation to shoot first and watched as he entered the 'bull'. Ellen went second and made sure her arrow was true. Turning at the very last minute, she loosed off the bolt and saw it pierce his heart.

In the kerfuffle that followed she made her escape, though she had never intended to be anything other than proud. In an age of debatable morals, men aroused by her bold act courted her. It was perhaps fitting that she should eventually marry Thomas 'Black' Vaughan.

CHRISTMAS

Herefordshire has plenty of custom and legend attached to this season of hope. We begin at Staunton-on-Wye.

A tale of the **oxen kneeling** as told to the Reverend Kilvert:

> I have known old James Meredith forty years and I have never known him far from the truth, and I said to him one day, 'James, tell me the truth, did you ever see the oxen kneel on old Christmas Eve at the Weston?' And he said, 'No, I never saw them kneel at the Weston but when I was at Hinton at Staunton-on-Wye I saw them. I was watching them on old Christmas Eve and at 12 o'clock the oxen that were standing knelt down upon their knees and those that were lying down rose up on their knees and there they stayed kneeling and moaning, the tears running down their faces.'   (Plomer 1944: pp. 323–4)

The national favourite of the **Blowing of the Thorn** touches Herefordshire as much as it does anywhere else. In Colwall, north-east of Ledbury, a particular thorn is said to blossom at midnight on old Christmas Eve (or Twelfth Night, if you follow the old Julian calendar). Several villages in the county maintain a similar claim, amongst them Stoke Edith and Ledbury.

'**Wassail, Wassail, all over the town** … ' conjures up images of Christmases past. The celebration in Huntington, Herefordshire was particularly intense, as reported in 1791 (reprinted in Leather, 2001):

A chain of fires, one large, twelve small, is set alight in the wheat fields of the parish, while cider is drunk and much hollering and shouting to drive away the evil spirits. The party in the next field answer in the same manner until the entire chain is 'alive'. A hearty supper follows, during which a 'boozy' cake – perfectly round with a hole in  its middle – is taken to the byre where the oxen are toasted, in good and strong ale. The cake is then placed on the horn of an ox, and the beast tickled into fits until he throws it off. If it should land to his rear, then the mistress of the house claims the cake; if to his fore, the bailiff! More pagan origins record a fertility rite: to the rear, failed crops, to the fore, a good harvest. Whatever the outcome, and whatever the meaning, more toasting seems essential to 'a happy new year':

> Here's to thee, Benbow, and to thy white horn,
> God send thy master a good crop of corn;
> Oh wheat, rye and barley, and all sorts of grain
> You eat your oats, I'll drink my beer
> May the Lord send us a happy new year!

Havergal (1887) records it in slightly different terms, mentioning Tretire near St Owen's Cross.

On St Stephen's Day ('modern' Boxing Day), the poor of Lyde parish (and others no doubt) called on the farms to seek a 'quartern' of wheat. This Gooding Day act befitted the season of goodwill.

LEGENDS

Just room for a couple:

The origins of the neighbouring villages of **Turnastone and Vowchurch** are fancifully recalled in the tale of two sisters who inherited land. One said unto the other: 'I vow to build my church, before you have turned a stone.' Hence the two neighbourly churches!

In the borderlands of Wales, the dragon myth appears in many Herefordshire villages, but few as spectacularly as the **Mordiford Wyvern** (winged dragon). He is still said to amble down from Haugh Wood to drink at the ford. It is based in large part on the tale of a young girl …

Set in medieval England, a lass known as Maud went out playing one day when along came a dragon and took her away. Or at least it took her heart. Keeping her secret, she fed him on milk, but before too much longer he fed on her ilk! And though local heroes were finally found, the young Maud wept loudly as it died on the ground.

This romantic tale is so beloved by the locals that for centuries a dragon was painted on the wall of Mordiford church.

CAKES OF PEACE

Pax cakes – Latin for peace – are still handed out at Easter in certain Herefordshire churches. Originally an annual opportunity to forgive past indiscretions, they follow the regular Christian habit of 'sharing the peace'. These cakes (or small buns) are distributed every Palm Sunday with the greeting 'Peace and Good Neighbourhood'. The churches of King's Caple, Hentland and Sellack all observe the custom dating back to the fifteenth century, when one wealthy worthy bequeathed bread and ale to his parishioners for the good of his soul.

THE INCREDIBLE MOVING HILL

Over three days in February 1575, Marcle Hill overlooking Much Marcle, shifted its position by 400yd! Like an earthquake, the ground shifted and yawed, consuming life and property as it went. Twenty-five acres were relocated by an event that still defies explanation. Two centuries later, the old chapel bell was found whilst a farmer was ploughing his field.

FEED THE SIN-EATER

It remained custom in nineteenth-century Herefordshire to pay the 'sin-eater' at funerals. Giving rise perhaps to the idea of the wake, a much feared but respected inhabitant of the district would be given food and drink as an act of swallowing the transgressions of the lately deceased.

One such, a 'long, lean lamentable' fellow, who lived in a cottage on the main road to Ross, received bread and ale passed over the coffin. As he ate, the dead inside were cleansed of their sins, free to move on, never to walk amongst the people again.

Unusually, the practise outlived the Reformation, when many such superstitions were so cruelly quashed.

8

A KIND OF MUSE

ARCHITECTURE

The county's architectural styles mix pastoral longevity with latter day ... erm ... blight? Yet even amidst the greatest architectural chaos, there are marvels – and quirks – to behold.

The **Herefordshire School of Romanesque** sculpture, a distinct twelfth-century movement, perfected by (overseas?) craftsmen, emerged at Hereford Cathedral. Known for it religious, though often-playful (even bawdy) carvings, the style is found in numerous churches, notably Kilpeck (see Religion – Churches, p.153), the Eardisley font, a ruinous Shobdon and the delightful St Michael's church, Castle Frome.

According to Harris (2006), Shobdon's newest St John the Evangelist 'is the only ecclesiastical example of the Rococo style of architecture in England' (2006: p. 316).

Now entombed by modernity, a seventeenth-century house on **Hereford's High Street** was moved out of the way during building work in 1965. Using rollers and tracks, the former apothecary shop was put back in place, forever obscured by its incongruous neighbours.

The Old House in Hereford is the solitary survivor of the seventeenth-century Butchers' Row. Now standing alone, it is 'fronted' by the nearby bronze Hereford Bull, cast to commemorate someone's love for the county (benefactor Clive Richards) and its gratitude to him. Note the Butchers Company Arms, high up on its south-western side.

Masonic Hall, Kyrle Street in Hereford stands on the site of the city's first public baths, founded by the Hereford Society for Aiding the Industrious. It was used first for washing (1853), then later for

swimming (1871–1927). Heat from a nearby steam mill warmed the water. Adjacent Bath Street takes its name from its once popular neighbour.

The **six gates of Hereford** (clockwise, from south): Wye Bridge, Friars, Eign, Widemarsh, Bye Street and St Owen's. Of these, only Friars' Gate probably existed before 1066.

ALMSHOUSES

These monuments to mercy are still found throughout the county. Major examples exist at:

St Katherine's Hospital, Ledbury – including a chapel and hall – began life in *c.* 1231, and was re-built *c.* 1330. Founded by Hugh Foliat, Bishop of Hereford, it was intended to cater to the needy and infirm. The surviving thirteenth-century chapel hosts one of Britain's oldest clocks! The adjacent Master's House (see p.30) was a sixteenth-century addition, home to the master of the nearby almshouses. An extra wing (of almshouses) was designed in 1867. Service buildings within the old precinct included 'barns, byres, malt houses and cider houses … kitchen, larder, cellar and warehouse, wash house, stable, cattle shed, byre, piggery, [and] barn' (source: Hereford Council).

Coningsby Hospital, Hereford – thirteenth-century origins, as the 'Hospital of the Holy Ghost and St John'. Later transferred to the Knights Hospitallers, it was re-founded in 1614 by Sir Thomas Coningsby, who added a new quadrangle and extensive new buildings. Now a local museum with chapel. (See also People – Nell Gwynne, p.65)

Pembridge has two sets of seventeenth-century black-and-white almshouses: Duppa's and Trafford's, each named after their founders. Of the former, four of the six still remain, while half a dozen of the latter survive to this day.

Cruxwell Street, Bromyard – seventeenth century, 'for the poor women of good character of the ancient township of Bromyard'. Seven original houses have since been converted into four 'flatlets'.

Rudhall's, Church Street, Ross-on-Wye – sixteenth century with much earlier foundations, a range of originally five (now three) tenement houses, built in red sandstone and two-storeyed. **Webb's Almshouses** on Copse Cross Street, a few years younger, use the same building material but have small pointed windows; established for seven poor men or women of the town.

BLACK-AND-WHITE VILLAGES (TRAIL)

The county boasts some of the best 'black-and-white' villages and towns in the country, so-called due to their distinctive architectural style … here are just three:

Eardisland
Quintessentially Herefordshire, set astride the River Arrow. Black-and-white, timber-framed houses, mostly sixteenth/seventeenth century.

Knapp House, Burton Court (originally a medieval great hall) and Staick House all date to the time of Edward III. The mound and moat of the former castle survive, as does the road over the river, reputedly followed by the future King Henry VII on his way to victory over Richard III at Bosworth Field.

Pembridge

A glorious triumph of Herefordshire black-and-white buildings, Pembridge boasts many claims to fame, not least its church. Set high on a 'tump' overlooking the Marches, its sturdy construction and arrow-slits betray its dual purpose as House of God and place of refuge. A violent past is further evidenced by the bullet-scarred west door – a victim of the Civil War. The detached bell house is thirteenth century, but its Scandinavian-inspired interior is quite out of place in rural England. Two sets of seventeenth-century almshouses display a more compassionate side.

Weobley

Weobley's history is as lengthy as its main street is wide. The open space at the south-western end – now complete with its modern magpie installation – has been watched over for eight centuries by the folk in this picturesque town. At either end are the symbols of power: to the south, the ramparts of a sizeable castle (see Borderlands – Castles); to the north, the church of St Peter and St Paul. The latter has the second tallest spire in the county.

MARKET HALLS/HOUSES

These seventeenth-century houses, found in the market towns of the county, were meeting places as well as centres of trade. Cherished examples survive at **Ledbury**, **Ross-on-Wye** and **Pembridge**.

Others, since lost, included **Leominster**, at the junction of High Street and Broad Street, pulled down in 1853, and **Kington**, dated 1654, demolished in 1768 – for overhanging the street! **Hereford**, *c.* 1600: this absolute gem was inexplicably demolished in 1862. It's upper storey was removed in 1792, due to the weight on its pillars. Once framed by Butchers' Row, also pulled down (see above), its demise was recorded as '[a] memorable piece of municipal vandalism' (Pevsner 1963).

(These three were likely built by John Abel, the King's Carpenter (1578/9–1675) – born, lived and buried at Sarnesfield.)

LITERATURE

(Other) Famous Authors And Poets (See Also Chapter 5)
William Langland, born *c.* 1330 in Colwall. Poet credited with the early medieval poem, 'Piers Plowman'. Written before the end of the 1300s, the narrator searches for the 'real' meaning of Christian life from his perspective of the Catholic faith. Some believe it is autobiographical. Written throughout using alliteration, it has been compared to Chaucer, to whom many credited the original work.

John Davies, poet and 'pen-man', 'the greatest master of the pen that England in her age beheld' (*ODNB*). Born Hereford *c.* 1564/5.

Thomas Newcomb, classical scholar and poet, born in the county *c.* 1681/2. Writer of odes to royalty, gentry and religious reform. Struggles with debt meant his days ended in a sorrowful state in Hackney in 1765. Supposedly great-grandson of Edmund Spenser.

Thomas Traherne, writer and cleric, born *c.* 1636. Son of a Hereford cobbler, he returned to the county as rector of Credenhill, before his death in Teddington, Middlesex in 1674. Regarded as one of the leading ecclesiastical writers and revered as a virtual saint in Hereford Cathedral (see Religion – Stained Glass in Herefordshire).

Chained Library
In the days when books were precious possessions, chaining collections became a matter of need. Dating from the 1600s, Hereford Cathedral's library is the oldest intact example in the world. The chained library at Oxford dates from roughly the same era, but lacks its original fixtures and fittings and thus authenticity.

Particular treasures at Hereford include: a reliquary supposedly depicting the murder of Thomas à Becket; an eighth-century collection of Anglo-Saxon gospels (its oldest work); and the earliest known drawing of an abacus, in a manuscript dated *c.* 1150. In the late twentieth century, the library grew, acquiring a second chained library, previously housed in nearby All Saints, and the library from Lady Hawkins' School, Kington (see p.115).

Magna Carta

In 1217, the young King Henry III (or, more accurately, his regents) issued a third version of his father's great charter, signed at Runneymede near Windsor on 15 June 1215. Though fundamentally unchanged, it contained updated clauses, and came complete with a new Charter of the Forest. This 1217 reissue is preserved in Hereford Cathedral, and played a significant part in the anniversary celebrations of Britain's democratic foundations.

Mappa Mundi

Included here for its contribution to literary history, this rare depiction of the medieval 'world' is one of Hereford's (and the country's) greatest treasures. Recording a thirteenth-century cleric's vision, it is less a map of the world – still thought to be flat – and more an extremely rare window into medieval minds.

The Holy Seat of Jerusalem lies at the centre, with east (the direction of the Second Coming) shown at the top. Biblical heartlands – including the Garden of Eden – form the religious depictions, while Adam and Eve, and the Tower of Babel, continue the biblical theme.

It also harbours many secular topics and pre-Christian features, such as the Labyrinth of Minos and the Colossus of Rhodes; a menagerie of beasts, from crocodile and rhino to elephant and bear; and (to modern eyes at least) fanciful icons of vampires and unicorns. A *sciapod* uses his gargantuan foot to shade from the sun!

Its author, Richard de Bello, treasurer of Lincoln Cathedral, became canon at Hereford (in or before *c*. 1305), explaining perhaps how it came to be here. Certainly, a later thirteenth-century date is quite likely, from the inclusion of Edward I's great castles at Caernarfon and Conwy, built at that time.

It was recently united with its original oak case, rediscovered in 1989.

Note: The Mappa Mundi and Chained Library are housed in the purpose-built New Library at Hereford Cathedral (opened 1996). Check times, displays and prices before visiting.

MUSIC

Three Choirs Festival

The Three Choirs Festival is the oldest classical music extravaganza in the world. Only two wars have interrupted the annual event since it first struck a chord, though its origins are now lost in time. Officially 1715, one source (Boden 1992) speculates it began a century earlier! Major performers have included Elgar (1890) and Vaughan Williams (1910).

Bringing together august choral traditions of the three great cathedrals – Hereford, Worcester and Gloucester – it began with just two services and a similar number of concerts. By the turn of the nineteenth century, when female singers were at last allowed to take part, it had grown to three days, finishing with an extravagant ball. The latest (2015) was hosted in Hereford, and lasted the now usual full week.

Sir Edward Elgar

Sir Edward is doubtless Herefordshire's most enduring musical icon. Born in 1857, in Worcestershire, his connection to Hereford was sealed in July 1904 (the year he was knighted) when he moved into Plas Gwyn, Hampton Park Road. He remained there for almost eight years, by which time his involvement with the city – the cathedral especially – was firmly established.

The son of a purveyor of sheet music, he was destined perhaps to pursue his chosen career. It brought him, however, both sorrow and joy.

Inspiration came in the beauty and peace of rural England, as he cycled its lanes and escaped the noise of the town. Still cutting his teeth, he earned money from teaching, but it was his work as a composer that cemented his fame.

Synonymous with The Last Night at the Proms, his *Pomp and Circumstance March No. 1* stirs many a heart, with its finale, *Land of Hope and Glory* – subsequently the crescendo at King Edward VII's coronation. His fervent patriotism had already been noted, in his *Imperial March* for Queen Victoria's diamond jubilee and *The Banner of St George*, his stirring cantata.

Yet Sir Edward was much more than fiercely English. His *Dream of Gerontius* is regarded as a choral colossus, while his *Enigma Variations*, heard every year at the Remembrance Day service, is the nation's most popular choice. Each variation reflects a relative or friend, one a favoured dog, and concludes with 'No. 14', his self-observation.

Today, he gazes *beyond* Hereford cathedral, a man resting in creative repose, as he leans on his trusty old bicycle and ponders perhaps his famous old quote: 'Music is in the air all around us.' A lasting reminder from Shropshire sculptress, Jemma Pearson.

PS – In an extra homage he would surely despise, the Elgar Trail is a 40-mile circular tour of some of his most redolent places, spread through the counties of Hereford and Worcester, devised by Worcester City and Malvern Hills district councils.

Other Musical Natives

Jenny Lind, opera soprano, aka 'The Swedish Nightingale'. Lived the last years of her life at Wynds Point in Colwall. Known for the purity of her voice and soul, her last public performance was at the Railway Servants' Benevolent Fund, Spa Hall, Malvern Hills, in 1883.

Mott the Hoople, 1960s/'70s rock group, famed for 'All The Young Dudes', penned by David Bowie. The only band ever supported on tour by Queen. Very much local (formerly named Silence), its members included natives of Hereford, Bromyard and Ross-on-Wye – Verden Allen, Dale Griffin, Ian Hunter, Mick Ralphs and Pete Overend Watts. They first signed to Island Records then, in 1972, to CBS.

The Pretenders, still fronted by Chrissie Hynde, sole survivor of the original line-up. Formed out of Hereford in 1978. By 1980, they achieved No. 1 in the UK Charts with 'Brass in My Pocket'. Original band members (with Hynde) were: James Honeyman-Scott, Pete Farndon and Martin Chambers, all lads from Hereford.

Ellie Goulding, established royal favourite. A native of Lyonshall and alumna of Lady Hawkins' School, Kington and Hereford Sixth Form College (see p.119). She famously played at the wedding reception of the Duke and Duchess of Cambridge (aka Prince William and Kate).

Mike Oldfield, eclectic musician, followed up his best-selling album *Tubular Bells* (1973) with a second, *Hergest Ridge* (1974). It was named after the Herefordshire landmark near to where he (then) lived.

It became his first number one album, remaining at the top for three weeks before being replaced by ... (for the first time) *Tubular Bells*!

THEATRE

David Garrick

Arguably the name synonymous with theatre, Garrick was the godfather of English acting. Born at the old Angel Inn, Widemarsh Street, in 1717, the world-famous performer and impresario had Huguenot blood.

He began his theatrical career via his writing, acting much later and then only in secret. By the mid-eighteenth century, however, he was firmly established in London's theatre land, and turned his sharp business mind to theatre management. Juggling the new demands with his appearances on stage, he gained international fame for his Shakespearian roles. Like the Kembles who followed, he helped place the Bard's works within reach of the people.

Most readily associated with Covent Garden and Drury Lane, the Garrick Theatre, Widemarsh Street, Hereford was built in 1882 (as the Theatre Royal) and re-named in honour of the great man in 1909 – more than a century after his death in 1779.

William Powell

Born and educated in eighteenth-century Hereford, Powell became a protégé of the mighty Garrick. He made his stage debut in 1793 at the Theatre Royal, Drury Lane, where the emotion he brought was welcomed in raptures. A prolific performer, he went on to develop a strong and life-long connection with Bristol, especially its King Street and Jacobs Well Theatre. After he died, suddenly, in 1769, he was buried in that city's cathedral, aged around 34.

The Kemble Ensemble

The Kemble acting dynasty, under the tutelage of Roger senior, stamped their indelible mark on the Herefordshire (and international) boards. Involvement began in the 1740s, through a certain John Ward, theatrical master, whose circuit of theatres included Hereford, Leominster, Warwick and Wales. After Roger Kemble married Sarah, Ward's daughter, he inherited the company, before extending its reach to several key towns across the Midlands and west.

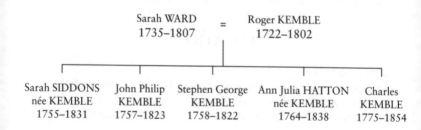

Sarah WARD 1735–1807 = Roger KEMBLE 1722–1802

Sarah SIDDONS née KEMBLE 1755–1831 | John Philip KEMBLE 1757–1823 | Stephen George KEMBLE 1758–1822 | Ann Julia HATTON née KEMBLE 1764–1838 | Charles KEMBLE 1775–1854

Born 1 July 1722 to a Hereford barber, Roger traded his scissors for costume and set out on an illustrious career in theatres, as far apart as Liverpool and Bath. Basing himself and his family in either Hereford and Worcester – according to season – Roger and Sarah soon nurtured a theatrical cast:

The birth of the first five of Roger's children, in five different towns, reveals the actor-theatre manager's itinerant life.

Their eldest child, Sarah (later **Sarah Siddons** – see p.70), drew hefty praise as the greatest actress of her age, especially for her tragic depictions. Perhaps more impressive was her ability to raise acting from a dubious pastime to respectable trade.

Her brother, **John Philip Kemble**, riding high on his sister's shoulders, became noted for his tragic and comic Shakespearian roles, while a third child, **Charles Kemble**, became a playwright, actor and theatre manager. Yet another, **Stephen George Kemble** – born in Kington, 1758 – pursued a similar path, most notably in Scotland and around the north-east.

In between, **Ann Julia Hatton**, herself an actor and writer, survived being shot through the eye and a later suicide bid in Westminster Abbey.

The Shakespearian 'tragic triumvirate' of Siddons, Kemble and George Frederick Cooke (or sister, brother and rival-cum-friend) achieved legendary status.

Herefordshire Theatres

The Hereford Courtyard opened in 1998 on the site of the old Nell Gwynne Theatre, itself opened in the former Municipal Baths (1979). It boasts a 436-seat main auditorium, 145-seat studio, visual arts galleries, meeting and function rooms, a rehearsal studio and the ubiquitous restaurant and bar. It also hosts the Kington Youth Theatre, reaching out to the far side of the county.

Bromyard's **Conquest Theatre** is perhaps the newest of its type, being established just over twenty years.

Phoenix Theatre, Ross-on-Wye; **Market Theatre**, Ledbury; and **Cawley Hall**, Leominster all deliver live entertainment.

Herefordshire Musical Theatre, which in 1898 was the Hereford Amateur Operatic Society, occupies Tomkins Theatre in Hereford's Whitecross Road.

Eighteenth-century **Leominster** once hosted a theatre in the Schoolhouse, intermittently used as a chapel and court.

Ross-on-Wye had a permanent theatre by 1829.

The Theatre in Broad Street, Hereford (now the site of Kemble House) held performances once every three years (though occasionally more often). Built in 1786, possibly replacing an earlier playhouse, it formed part of Kemble's circuit, by then run by a John Bowles Watson. In 1857, it gave way to the Corn Exchange, which in 1911 became the Kemble Theatre. In 1963, when that too was demolished, films and even a roller-skating rink could not prevent its demise.

Theatrical Tragedy

In 1916, the **Garrick Theatre** on Widemarsh Street suffered a hideous fire. Eight young girls, performing a charity show, lost their lives to a tragedy of disputable cause. Raising funds for First World War soldiers, the cotton wool costumes the children were wearing caught fire and burned in a flash. A rogue match from a smoker was instantly cited, though the inquest held later failed to pinpoint the truth.

A heritage plaque marks the site – now a municipal car park – though moves are afoot for a more fitting memorial.

9

EDUCATION
AND LANGUAGE

In 1148, when Robert de Bethune, Bishop of Hereford and advocate
for educating the young, suddenly died, he took with him any dim hope
of education for all. And it took 700 years for four Acts of Parliament
and one Royal Commission to ensure all children younger than 12
attended a school:

1870   Elementary Education Act – to provide a school in locations
       where there were none
1876   Royal Commission on the Factory Acts – recommended
       compulsory education as an alternative to child labour
1880   Elementary Education Act – compulsory education for 5 to 10
       year olds
1893   Elementary Education (School Attendance) Act –
       extended attendance to 11 years of age
1899   Act amended – leaving age raised to 12

EMINENT HEREFORDSHIRE SCHOOLS

Education of the county's young can be traced back for some to the
Norman arrival, and possibly even sooner. Herefordshire's most
prominent schools were at the very beginning of a long and, at times,
arduous path to self-improvement.

Bishop of Hereford's Bluecoat School
Since its inception in 1552, the famous Bluecoat School movement –
in reality, a loosely connected family of charity schools – has educated
children within its core Christian values. Established by Edward VI
(r. 1547–53), at Christ's Foundling Hospital in Greyfriars, London
it was named after the traditional long coats worn by the pupils, belted
at the waist and considered by some to be the first of its type.

Hereford school, founded in 1710, occupied the building still seen at the site of the old Bye Street Gate (Bluecoat Street, or inner ring road). It moved later to the old High School buildings in Widemarsh Street, and today it is located at Tupsley.

Ross-on-Wye Bluecoat School

Originated in 1717, for thirty boys and the same number of girls. From 1799, the school sat in Walter Scott House (Old Gloucester Road), named after its benefactor, former pupil and famed local worthy. Coming back to the town, he discovered his old school in decay and rallied its fortunes with a considerable bequest. In 1835, it clothed sixty pupils, at a cost of £95 7s 6d. (Source: Toplis, A. 2011, *The Clothing Trade in Provincial England: 1800–1850*)

Leominster Free School

Endowed by Queen Mary (r. 1553–58), it was situated in an ancient chapel dedicated to the Virgin Mary.

Lady Hawkins School, Kington

Established in 1632 through the will of Lady Hawkins, wife of the cousin of Sir Francis Drake and herself one of the Vaughans of Hergest Court. The school building was designed by John Abel, King's Carpenter (see Architecture), while its purpose was 'for the instructing and teaching of youths and children in literature and good education'. Its historic collection of literature and books is now an adjunct to the Chained Library at Hereford Cathedral (see p.107). (Source: www.lhs. hereford.sch.uk)

Lucton School, Near Leominster

John Pierrepoint, successful London vintner, endowed a school for the boys of his native rural north Herefordshire. Opened in 1708 in the purpose-built home it occupies today, three centuries later it is a co-educational school. The glorious original Queen Anne building has been enhanced by Victorian and later additions – of a scale Pierrepoint could never have dreamed.

Cathedral School, Hereford

Of uncertain antiquity, the school is in any case old. Founded by the Lateran Council and its Edict of 1179 – or, some say, by Bishop Gilbert, 200 years later – the sons (and, since 1970, daughters) of families all over the world, have been taught in the shadow of Hereford Cathedral. It was certainly Gilbert who appointed Richard of Cornwall headmaster in 1384, bringing to an end the abnegation of Holy Scripture and education for boys. And his responsibilities were couched in unequivocal language:

> master for rule and government of the Grammar School with rod and birch, in accordance with custom for one year only (in Moir 1964: p. 31).

In 1583, ahead of a resurgence in fortunes, it was made a **Free Grammar School,** so called because Latin and Greek were taught gratis, though the master could charge for anything else. Not until 1853 was it known as the **Cathedral School,** when choristers were taught in return for duties performed in the cathedral choir.

The school buildings, meanwhile, followed a similar path: Under Edward VI (r. 1547–53), a new structure plausibly replaced an older precursor, while Charles I (r. 1625–49), royal benefactor to the city, granted a house and garden on what, to this day, is the School House and Yard.

A new, enlarged school was constructed in 1760–62, possibly on the same site as before. Set within the Bishop's Cloister, it overlooked Lady Arbour and the Palace Yard; and, loosely re-christened 'the Music Room', hosted other activities, including the Three Choirs Festival.

After it too was pulled down, from 1835 lessons were taught at the headmaster's house, until rooms in the College of the Vicars Choral were used as a temporary measure.

Since 1875, the school has remained on the site of the old Canon's Bakehouse to the rear of School House. And the number of places comprising its campus has swelled from just one to a magnificent seven. Gathered around Castle Street and the Close, they are augmented by 'satellite' sites, such as the Wyeside playing fields off Broomy Hill.

(Information taken from Anon n.d. and (with permission) of Tomlinson n.d. – www.herefordcs.com/history, accessed August 2015)

Selected Rules of the School (1808)

1 Every boy must be in his place from a quarter after seven till nine; half-past nine till eleven; twelve till two; three till five.
2 Every boy shall be furnished with a pen-case, containing at all times not less than three pens, slate pencil, and a lead pencil, and also a pen-knife. A boy not having these requisites, together with a slate lined by him during school hours, shall be reported by the Assistant Teacher to the Master, and receive a cut on his hand. The boys in the junior classes are not to have penknives, unless ordered to procure them.
3 A boy leaving his book out of its place forfeits one half-penny.
4 All the boys when a Master shall come into school shall rise, and stand until he has taken his seat, or desires them to sit down. If a stranger shall come in, each class shall rise as he passes them, and then sit down and proceed with their work as if no one more than usual were present.
5 Any boy writing on the walls, cutting the desks, doors, or rails in the Churchyard shall transcribe a sermon.
6 Whatever benches or windows may be broken, or other damage done, shall be repaired by those who do it, if they can be discovered, or otherwise by the general fund to be raised by subscription among the boys.
7 All games are prohibited in the Churchyard, which may endanger the Church windows or disturb the service of the Church.
8 All lying, swearing, or prophaning (*sic*) the name of God shall invariably be punished with a flogging.
9 All cruelty to animals shall be severely punished.
10 A boy shall not pass a Master out of School without touching his hat.
11 Dirty hands or face or holes in the clothes shall be punished by a cut on the hand for each, and if this will not arrest the sloven, this name shall be affixed to his back in large letters.
12 If a boy retain anything in his possession belonging to another, he shall receive for the first offence three cuts on the hand, for the second six, and for every succeeding offence a flogging or expulsion.

(Source: Carless 1914)

Prospectus (1913)
Outdoor activities were an important part of life at the school:

Boating – the regular exercise of senior boys during the Lent term, in which the School Regatta and Inter-School Boat Races take place. In the Summer Term there are many opportunities of exploring the beautiful reaches of the Wye ... No boy is allowed the use of Boats until he has obtained a Swimming Certificate.
Cricket and Football* – At Wyeside, adjoining the River, the School possesses a field of ten acres, which has at great expense been made into one of the best Cricket Grounds in the West of England.
Fives – There are two Fives Courts in the Playground.
Military Drill – All boys over 13 years of age belong to the OT (Officer Training) Corps, and special attention is given to Musketry Training.
Natural History – There is a Museum in process of formation, and Nature Study is encouraged by meetings for papers and discussion throughout the year, by Natural History Outings in the Summer Term, and by prizes annually for Collections.

[*Previously considered 'a low game, only to be indulged in by boys of an inferior grade']

(Source: Carless 1914)

Cathedral Preparatory School
Founded in 1898 and housed in the same building for the past ninety years, it was incorporated into the Cathedral School and renamed the Junior School for pupils aged 11 and under.

THE ROYAL NATIONAL COLLEGE FOR THE BLIND

In 1872, an idea for The Royal Normal College and Academy for the Blind was realised by Victorian physician, Dr Thomas Rhodes Armitage, and American music master, Francis Joseph Campbell, himself blind since 5 years of age. ('Normal' referred to the regular teaching methods, something that until then had been lacking for children with little or no sight.)

Campbell escaped persecution (and possible hanging) from those who despised his anti-slavery stance! Saved only by a popular sympathy for his visual impairment, he later met Armitage and the pair plotted the school.

The college began life at Crystal Palace and then Upper Norwood, both in London, before pupil numbers demanded a far grander site. By 1939, though, it was forced into a peripatetic existence with the outbreak of war. Indeed, within twenty-four hours, it had decamped to Aylesbury in Bucks, and the old premises were left to the pounding from enemy bombs.

Now faced with insurmountable hurdles, it closed for a while, another hidden victim of Hitler's intent. Salvation came in Rowton Castle near Shrewsbury, but a fierce fire razed most of the buildings and the college was once again back on the road.

Finally, in 1978, it founded its Hereford campus, between College Road and Venns Lane where it remains to this day. The main, grandiose building, a former Hereford college of teacher training erected in 1902, offered an ideal opportunity for some overdue stability in a challenging world.

SOME OTHER COLLEGES IN THE COUNTY

Agriculture and Tech
From its post-war origins as **Hereford Technical College** – teaching blacksmiths and farriers and housed on Newtown Road in the city – the **Herefordshire and Ludlow College of Further Education** has moved into Folly Lane, Hereford. Following a £32 million redevelopment programme, completed in 2010, the modern campus includes a site out at Holme Lacy dedicated, in this most rural of counties, to studying the land. (Source: www.hlcollege.ac.uk.

Arts
Part of the Folly Lane development, **Hereford College of Arts** opened its doors as the Hereford College of Art and Design in 1851! Its two campuses – the other is in the old County College (see RNCB) – provide education and inspiration in all forms of art. Providing social cohesion through its non-educational facilities, it is an established part of the county. (Source: www.hca.ac.uk and others)

Hereford Sixth Form College
Itself part of the Folly Lane estate, established in 1973, and covering Herefordshire and surrounds, it 'offers a broad, general education in a caring and supportive environment which enables you to gain the qualifications you need to enter higher education or employment'. (Source: www.hereford.ac.uk)

NB: other schools, colleges and academies are available.

A UNIVERSITY FOR THE TWENTY-FIRST CENTURY

Herefordshire's famed lack of a university (one of only three counties in England to suffer that scar) is optimistically set to improve. A grand opening planned for 2017 will reveal Britain's first 'green field' university for thirty years.

Offering a wide range of degree-level subjects, the breadth of which are caught in its name – the **New Model Institute for Technology and Engineering** (NMITE) – its focus will be on STEM tuition (science, technology and maths), an apparently struggling sector, despite our 'technological' age. Based in an eclectic mix of existing buildings and sites spread right through the town, the first university since Buckingham in 1974 is the brainchild of philosopher A.C. Grayling.

LANGUAGE

Like many rural shires, Herefordian dialects, phrases and sayings endure to enthral …

Advice on the weather
'The nearer to twelve in the afternoon, the drier the moon;
The nearer to twelve in the forenoon, the wetter the moon.'

The clouds over Penyard Hill (near Bollitree) are known locally as 'Old Penyard smoking his pipe'. Apparently, if he puffs away in the morning, there'll be rain before night.

Advice when alive
'Bread when you're hungry, drink when you're dry;
Rest when you're weary, and heaven when you die.'

Sayings to live by
'I couldn't cut rumps of beef out of mouse's legs' – living within your means!
'I'm all *avoirdurpoised*' – unsure about something
'Backwards and forwards' – there's nothing else to say
'He's as useless as a midsummer gosling' – ill, insipid, as the young geese who stagger and go weak in the sun
'I suffer with brownkites' – bronchitis
'I saw him bespoke' – he looked near to death

'Fettle' – feed or 'bed up' cattle; to put in good order, as in 'fine fettle'
'Bug's words' – boasting
'She's a deawbeater' – she walks with her toes turned out
''e be a bye blow' – he is of questionable birth
'Why can't you be up in the day, instead of hooleting about the country?' –
  nocturnal, like an owl
'As silk as a hoont' – smooth, like a mole, often used for a well-groomed horse
'Gone with mother a-chattin'' – gathering 'chips', a common excuse for
  truancy from school
'It do fair quop' – it's throbbing with pain
'We're all in a mullock' – what a mess!
'My eyebrows, they itch' – I sense a visitor comes calling

Some unusual nouns
'A lawter of eggs' – the number laid before sitting
'Bloody fingers' – foxgloves
'Bottle-Tit' – long-tailed titmouse, after the shape of its nest; also called
  a *Mum-ruffian*
'Bum-bailiffs' – sheriff's officer
'Bussock', 'Jubbin' – donkey
'Cockhoop' or 'Pink' – bullfinch
'Deadman' – scarecrow
'Deathzear' – first twelve months after a family bereavement
'Fluttermouse' – bat
'Free-martin' – one of twin heifers, always thought to be barren
'I'll gee thee a lowk on thy 'ead!' – I'll give you a lump!
'Ladies' lap dog' – destructive grub feeding on hops
'Lommaking' – making love (or idle and clumsy) – surely not related!
'Minty cheese' – cheese riddled with mites
'Mouzend' – end of the month following a funeral
'Quakers' – not the religious folk, but stitchwort or quaking grass
'Scruffy urchin' – hedgehog
'Seven coloured linnet' – goldfinch
'Stockeagle' – Green Woodpecker
'Veldey-bird' – fieldfare
'Wig' – cake or bun, especially around Leominster
'With this logger … ' – wedding ring

Some words recorded in 1804
'Cantle' – a piece of bread or cheese
'Daffish' – embarrassed or easily abashed
'Gawn' – a gallon
'Gib' – a castrated tom

'Glat' – a gap in a hedge
'Plock' – a small meadow
'Scog' – to boast
'Tollet' – a hayloft

(Source: Duncumb 1804)

Finally, some rhymes about people and places
'Dirty Cowarne, wooden steeple,
Crak'd bell, wicked people.'

'Hope under Dinmore and if Dinmore should fall
The Devil will have Hope and Dinmore and All.'

'Lusty Tarrington, lively Stoke
Beggars at Weston, Thieves at Woolhope.'

'"A dish and a spoon," say the bells of Bish Frome
"Trip a trap a trencher," say the bells of Lemster
"Come old man and shave yer beard," say the bells of Bromyard
Poor Weobley, proud people, low church, high steeple.'

WELSH ORIGINS

The impact of the Welsh language on place names in Herefordshire is well understood:

Ergyng (*Arcenfelde*, Archenfield) – the Welsh enclave (commote, *cwmwd*)
Ewias (Ewyas), as in E. Harold, E. Lacy (now Longtown) – sheep district
Dinedor – fort (*din*) on a hill (*bre*)
Doward (Little and Great) – *dwy-garth* or two heights
Ganarew – *genau rhiw*, hill pass
Great Corras – corruption of *rhos*, meaning moor or heath
Hentland – *hen-llan* or old church

Llan – church land (enclosure) (of a saint) ... as in the following:
   cillo – of St Sulfyw
   cloudy – unidentified saint? (corruption of *Llanllowdy* or *Loncleudi*?)
   dinabo – unidentified saint or *Inabwy*, former Bishop of Llandaff
   garron – on the Garren river
   gunnock – Cynog, son of Brychan Brycheiniog (as in Brecon)
   warne – by the alder swamp

Mynyddbrydd – speckled mountain
Penallt (King's Caple) – hill top or cliff head*
Pencoyd (pencoed) – end of the wood
Pengethley (pen-celli) – head of a grove
Tre – either truncation of *tref* (from *cantref*, Welsh administrative unit) or *tre* (town, village, homestead)
Yazor – Iago's ridge, from the Welsh Iago (Jacob), or Old English for yew ridge
Welsh Newton, found before you reach Monmouth and Wales.

(Source: greatly informed by *Herefordshire Place-names*, Coplestone-Crow 2009, Lias 1991 and Bannister 1916)

*Noted as the one purely Welsh place name on the English side of the Wye (below Hereford) (Bannister).

10

ECONOMY

BUSINESS & TRADE

Herefordshire's wealth has come from the land, surprising given its ancient infertile nature and the great tracts of 'waste' from the wars with the Welsh. Today, it aims to be the country's largest producer of food – and especially drink. (NB: inclusion here is not an endorsement; other brands do exist.)

Cider
Easily the county's most recognisable export, from some world-famous producers:

Bulmers (now part of the Heineken group) – its factory in Hereford is the largest in Europe. Founded in 1887 by Henry Percival (H.P.) Bulmer, son of the Credenhill rector, his business soon occupied the site of the present Cider Museum (Ryelands Street). In the late 1970s, it moved to Plough Lane where, in 2003, it was sold to Scottish & Newcastle (subsequently bought by the Carlsberg & Heineken Group in 2008). Its main cider, Strongbow, still accounts for half of the nation's total cider consumption.

Westons, Much Marcle – founded by Henry Weston in 1878, still working out of Bounds Farm. One of the first cider factories and still family-run, its famous Old Rosie refers to their 1921 steamroller, named after Laurie Lee's *Cider with Rosie*.

Dunkertons Organic Cider – produced near Pembridge, has used its own pressings (of apples and pears) since 1980. Still very much a family business.

Symonds Cider (1727–1984) – claimed to be the oldest cider-makers in the county, they introduced the eponymous label, 'Scrumpy Jack'. Based at Bodenham before Mr Bill Symonds moved lock, stock and barrel across to Stoke Lacy. Now too part of the Heineken stable.

Potatoes
Now a staple of Herefordshire farms, its local importance has grown since 2001 and the start of Tyrrells of Stretford Bridge, near Leominster. Founded by farmer, Will Chase, it originally used only potatoes grown on the farm. Today, it prides itself on using county-grown spuds – and on its humorous packaging.

Milk
Since 1936, Cadbury's processing centres, such as the one at Marlbrook near Leominster, have consumed vast quantities of Herefordshire milk in producing their world-famous confectionery.

Poultry
A battery of sheds reveals both the chicken and egg are the modern-day giants of Herefordshire trade. Once locally synonymous with Sun Valley, poultry processing in Hereford still accounts for around 2 million chickens a week. Two city sites continue to thrive.

Sheep
Another staple economy in the county! The Ryeland sheep in particular were much prized for their luxurious wool, while the Archenfield and Leominster flocks were so well regarded that the latter was labelled the 'Leominster Ore'. In the mid-fifteenth century, its wool was selling for £13 per sack or £1 per tod – six times its value from the sheep bred in Sussex.

Until the end of the last millennia, the Clun Forest flock were still lambed in the ancient Tithe Barn at Stockton Bury.

Bulls
The world-famous Hereford Bull (see p.43) can be found right around the world: giving rise to the second burgeoning export, bull semen.

Soft Fruits
Herefordshire has exported blackcurrants since the seventeenth century, when they were packed in ice and sent down the Wye and on to London. Windmill Hill Fruits at Harewood End is a main player.

Other (Non-food)

When you buy plants for the garden, there's a good chance they were grown at Herefordshire's Allensmore Nurseries, which began life in the 1970s as a local, family-run firm.

Pontrilas Sawmills have grown since 1947 into the largest sawmill in the Western world. Started after the war by John R. Hickman, his family still run the business, albeit along more modern lines.

GUILDS

The Guilds, a Saxon custom for the 'distribution of reparations and enforcement of belonging and public good', became a form of Trade Association, preventing non-members selling within the city or town. Amongst the most ancient in Hereford were: 'carpenters, corvisiers, bovvyers, fletchers, cardmakers, saddlers, fullers, tailors, butchers, blacksmiths, bakers, mercers, glovers, goldsmiths, barbers, dyers, tanners, chandlers, cordwainers, pewterers, cutlers, harpers, plumbers, pin-makers, makers of bow-strings, arrow-head makers, makers of parchment, glaishers, braishers and *motley weavers*' (Johnson 1882).

MILLS & BOOM

The corn mills were grinding up to 1,000 bushels a week, their fulling contemporaries employing carders, weavers, fullers, walkers and spinners.

The mills on the Wye, especially those around Hereford, enjoyed historic success until King Henry VIII (r. 1509–47) sent orders for their total destruction: ' [In] a private letter from the king [obtained] by sinister mean ... the four mills were thrown down and destroyed', said to have come from 'a wrongful suggestion made ... upon malice borne to the dean and chapter [of Hereford Cathedral].' (Source: Johnson 1882)

ANOTHER ROUND

Cider was not always the icon of mass-production. Its importance to local farms and estates remains evident in the number of old presses tucked away on the farms.

Local Presses
Historic examples survive at:

- Hellens, Much Marcle
- Gwatkins, Abbey Dore
- Orgasmic Cider, Eardisley
- Lower Norton Farmhouse, Brockhampton
- Stockton Bury (see Gardens), where the press was mentioned after the Dissolution, but was probably in existence before

Orchards (See Also Chapter 3)
Huge crops are now grown to meet modern demand, though some retain traditional methods. Despite a 40 per cent reduction in number, there remain over *c.* 3,000 spread over the county. Here are a few:

(Please note: many of those listed are private. For orchard walks on permissive paths, go to www.news.herefordshire.gov.uk/leisure/)

- Henhope, Priors Frome
- Tidnor Wood, near Lugwardine
- Lady Close, Bodenham Lake Nature Reserve
- Half Hyde, Bishop's Frome
- Salt Box, Garnons
- Village Plum, Glewstone
- Standard Farm, Moccas
- Monnington with Brobury, south of the Roman road
- Kingstone and Madley

(Source: Robertson *et al.*, 2012 and www.herefordorchards.co.uk)

11

TRANSPORT

From ferries to canals, tram roads to trains, from straight Roman highways to meandering lanes, Herefordshire has proved itself able to move with the times – except during rush hour!

FERRIES

Twenty-five hand ferries once criss-crossed the Wye, from Chepstow in the south to Ross-on-Wye in the north. Only two now remain – outside the Old Ferrie Inn and the Saracen's Head. The famed **Huntsham Ferry**, farther upstream, was replaced by a bridge, though signs of its use are still to be found. (Sources: www.yeoldferrieinn.com and www.htt. herefordshire.gov.uk)

An oar ferry operated at **Whitney-on-Wye**, charging a penny a time. It has since been replaced by the toll bridge of 1799 (see p.172). In time immemorial, the ferryman was murdered for his takings, leading to two men being hanged (see p.143).

A horse ferry at Hoarwithy Passage – 'ye greate passage Boote of Horewethie' – was the only means of crossing the Wye until the bridge of 1856–57 was constructed (since replaced). (Source: www.bosci.net)

Other ferries recorded:

Mancell's Ferry between Fownhope and Ballingham
Wilton Bridge near Ross-on-Wye
Ferry and cottage at Kerne Bridge
Bycross Ferry at Preston-on-Wye.

(Source: www.herefordshire.gov.uk)

CANALS

Herefordshire's two canals, the **Hereford & Gloucester** and the **Leominster to Stourport**, were both engineering marvels – and both destined to fail. The florescence of the canals, in the late eighteenth century, accessed new markets for local produce and goods. In Herefordshire, cider, limestone and coal – by linking Wales with the Midlands – could have brought wealth to the west.

Yet, calling to mind the old bargee's adage that 'a boat is a hole in the water into which you pour cash', the canals soon proved nothing more than sinking ships …

The Hereford & Gloucester

Work began at Gloucester as early as 1793, but it took five years before reaching the border. The Oxenhall Tunnel – a dedicated, 1¼-mile section between Ledbury and Newent – drained scarce resources, requiring twenty airshafts and thousands of bricks. When a second tunnel was needed, this time at Ashperton, only time and a cartload of money averted disaster after the structure started to slump.

When the canal finally reached Hereford, in May 1845, it had taken more than fifty years to complete. By then, it was no longer needed – the new wonders of rail had begun to arrive!

In the end, the Hereford & Gloucester lasted just forty years, closing completely in 1885. To add insult to injury, much of its bed was leased to GWR (Great Western Railway), who laid down their Gloucester to Ledbury line where the canal should have been.

Leominster to Stourport

The Leominster to Stourport fared even worse. Protracted negotiations delayed the start from its inception in 1789 until a proposed link to Kington was finally approved. The extended 'cut', of some 46 miles, came with a colossal budget of £150,000.

Perhaps due to the complicated engineering solutions – four tunnels, three aqueducts and innumerable locks – great parts of the route were never created. In fact, barely 20 miles were ever dug, chiefly from Leominster to the coal pits at Mamble.

Disaster, though, was never afar and, in 1795, the new Southnet Tunnel completely collapsed. Never repaired, it is still claimed two workmen and their boat remain buried inside.

The end now was in sight, and a string of rescue schemes – including tram roads laid on the bed and with them new finance – all came to naught. By the time it was sold, in 1848, the original investors had seen their capital shrink by 85 per cent.

PS: Many archaeological finds have been made during excavation of the county's canals. During aqueduct works (1842) to carry the Hereford & Gloucester over the Frome, black soil, faunal material, Roman artefacts, a bronze spearhead and gold jewellery were all recovered.

RIVERS

For a county well defined by its rivers, a lively trade in goods and passengers was inevitable. But soon easy passage was hindered amidst a plethora of economic concerns, designed to harness its power and abundance of fish. From mills to weirs, fish-traps to quays, the Rivers Wye & Lugg Navigation Act 1696 brought only temporary improvement.

The **Wye**, at 157 miles long, is Britain's fifth longest river. The above Act sought to open up its potential downstream of Glasbury. However, even today, larger craft are restricted to its lower reaches near Chepstow, while only pleasure craft are seen farther upstream.

The **Lugg**, once opened up beyond Leominster through the same legislation, has remained similarly impeded. Despite several attempts, such as flash locks (which allow boats to pass while weirs or mills are still working), the river never fulfilled its potential for trade. Commerce ceased as far back as the nineteenth century, and only leisure pursuits continue today.

Loads once carried on the Lugg included timber, pig iron, coal, clay (for pots and bricks), paper, slate, lime, bricks and food.

The locks, more readily connected with the man-made canals, were used on the river, some of which are still visible today. Examples were known at Mordiford (where the Lugg meets the Wye), Tidnor, near Hereford, and by Hampton Court Castle. But the fish traps and weirs still hindered the traffic and, in 1727, a third River Wye & Navigation Act demanded their end.

Wharfs were another obstruction, though these centres of trade at least saw cargoes unloaded and markets supplied. One, in Hereford, sat alongside the river, beneath Castle Green. Its former presence is recorded in Quay Street, running up to Castle Street and the cathedral.

Ross Dock was part of the commercial and aesthetic development of the town, inspired by Kyrle (see p.66) and included Wye Street (formerly Dock Pitch).

RAIL

The following owes much to Leslie Oppitz's excellent history of the *Lost Railways of Herefordshire and Worcestershire* (see bibliography). The map at the front of Oppitz's book shows extant rail routes as a solid line, those long since removed by a series of dots. To the west and south, between Newport, Shrewsbury and Birmingham – essentially the whole of Herefordshire – the plan resembles a child's dot-to-dot drawing. Seen like this, we can't help but to lament the county's lost railway heritage and its connections to the rest of the world.

Tramways
These horse-drawn carriageways connected the Usk coalfields and lime quarries of Kington to the markets of Hereford and Hay-on-Wye. In 1829, one of the first of its kind linked the city with Abergavenny.

Early Doors
The driving force for progress was not people but goods. Freight movements, even by tram, were proving too slow, and Stephenson, Brunel and the others pushed on with their new efficient, steam-powered system of travel by train.

Broad or Narrow?
Brunel's Great Western Railway (GWR) was constructed using the so-called broad gauge – 7ft ¼in – heading eastward from Bristol till it met its rivals on the emerging nationwide grid: the narrow gauge – of no more than 3ft 6in – had already given way to the standard (4ft 8½in) by the time the line from Shrewsbury reached Hereford in 1853.

The industrial heartlands and busy ports in the north were being linked with the rich coalfields and traders in the south. Brunel accepted that his lines had to change.

Celebrations

Hereford was the last major city to be connected by rail. Accordingly, on 6 December 1853, the townspeople held a spectacular fete to celebrate the late arrival of steam. An earlier, failed attempt – to welcome the first ever train on the Shrewsbury & Hereford Railway (S&HR) – was quickly forgotten, as the first service on the new Newport, Abergavenny & Hereford Railway (NA&HR) drew a much prouder response.

Up to 60,000 people flocked to the city, half that number lining the track! Marching bands and a grand banquet at Shire Hall saw festivities last well into the night, when the gas jets were lit and a light show begun. Each civic building, from workhouse to pubs, theatre to Town Hall, played its role in displaying the universal pride of the town. And not even the late arrival of that very first train dampened the mood!

Note: fuller accounts have been given elsewhere (e.g. www.htt.herefordshire.gov.uk).

Lost Railways of Herefordshire

From August 1857, trains ran along the **Leominster & Kington Railway** (L&KR), a line stretching from Leominster in the east to Kington in the west, replacing the horse-drawn tramway of 1820. It would not last a century, though, and closed in 1957.

Opening in 1874, the **Kington & Eardisley Railway** (K&ER) picked up the baton, running services south to Eardisley junction. It included a short branch via Titley and on to Presteigne.

In the northern reaches, centred on Little Hereford, the **Tenbury & Bewdley Railway** had been built along the bed of the Leominster Canal. GWR worked the line, which ran through three counties: from Woofferton in Shropshire, through Herefordshire's Easton Court, to the far end at Bewdley in Worcestershire. Opened in sections from 1861, it closed in similar stages just a century later.

The **Worcester, Bromyard & Leominster Railway** (WB&LR) was given life in the 1861 Parliamentary Act. The full plans, however, only saw light on 1 September 1897: a portentous delay. For more than a decade, built in separate sections from either end of the line, the two halves would never meet in the middle. Instead, the two lengths were closed in similar fashion: from 1952 to Beeching's cuts of the 1960s, it was slowly dismantled, one piece at a time. The WB&LR thus became known as the 'unfinished line'.

The **Hereford, Hay & Brecon Railway** (HH&BR) linked the coalfields of South Wales to the markets of Hereford and Worcester. First opened to goods traffic leaving Hereford in 1862, two years later it reached its most westerly point in the county, north-east of Hay. The HH&BR joined forces with the Brecknock & Abergavenny Canal but, like the L&KR (see above), it could never survive. It finally shut in its 100th year.

Ross-on-Wye once dreamed of having two lines: the **Ross & Ledbury** and the **Ross & Monmouth**. The former was abandoned for a new through route, the 'Daffodil Line', which opened between Gloucester and Ross in 1885. It survived until 1964, though by then only to freight. **The Monmouth & Ross** (via Symonds Yat) opened to passenger traffic in 1873, lasting a full ninety years before it, too, felt the axe.

The **Hereford, Ross & Gloucester Railway** (HR&GR) linked these three major centres, joining up with the neighbouring lines. It began operations in 1855, but was subsumed within seven years by GWR. A century later, it closed to all traffic, but can be followed in part by horse or on foot.

The Golden Valley Railway

The Golden Valley railway linked Dorstone to the line at Pontrilas, the latter operated by GWR who opposed the new scheme. That should have been read as an omen.

The new line was agreed in 1876, with an extension to Hay quickly proposed. Opening five years later, and though still unwelcome to many, the first train was celebrated in spectacular fashion at the Boughton Arms pub, Peterchurch. The great and the good arrived on specially hired trains, and Abbey Dore, Bacton, Vowchurch, Peterchurch and Dorstone were at long last connected. The connection to Hay, though – another bad omen – had failed to start.

After only four years, passenger numbers had missed expectations and the loss-making line was temporarily closed. The still absent Hay branch was adjudged to be crucial: without it, the line was a flop. Yet, months later, reopen it did, and for a while somehow kept going. Then, in 1889, the new line to Hay was finally completed and with it came a new era of hope.

It was not to be, however. By 1892, with debts mounting and no agreements with carriers, its creditors sequestered the trains – despite the GVR Board locking level crossings, attempting to prevent their removal.

Yet the perennial phoenix rose up once again, this time surviving for a further five years. But disaster returned, when the extension from Dorstone to Hay was condemned as unsafe. By Spring 1898, the entire line had closed down.

GWR, its one-time opponent, now came to the rescue – re-laying the track and installing new stock. Trains once again ran through the valley by 1901. For nearly four decades, until the outbreak of war, they kept the service alive. Yet even this was not the end of the line. With a new depot at Elm Park, the line was now used by the wartime Ministry of Supply.

At the end of the war, the old problems appeared, and in 1957 the Golden Valley line finally closed. The track was torn up and most of the stations dismantled. Those who had opposed it from the very beginning now cast an unsavoury smirk.

Lost Stations
Long before the closure of lines, many of the stations had fallen foul of the times. Platforms, ticket halls, lights, even clocks disappeared from view or fell into ruin. Many an overgrown remnant can still be found – if you know where to look …

Hereford once had three stations, of which Hereford **Barr's Court** is the single survivor. The others were **Moorfields** (HH&BR), on the north side of Eign Street–Whitecross Road (opposite Ryelands Street); and **Barton** (NA&HR), to the south nearby (Grimmer Road). Both closed in 1979, each only handling goods traffic since 1874 and 1893.

The line leaving **Vowchurch Station** is barely visible as a slight rise on the Turnastone road.

Kingsland Station is preserved in the railway cottage, now a private residence, where the line once crossed the busy A4110.

Rowden Mill, north-west of Bromyard, must be the jewel in the crown of old Herefordshire stations. Very much a private endeavour, the owners have restored the buildings, platforms, lighting and even a diesel saloon, which sits on the track awaiting ghosts from the past.

The **Bulmer Railway Centre** once stood as part of Hereford Moorfields (see above). From 1968, for barely three decades, it was an operational lifeline, and a test-bed for rail as an alternative to road. Its famed locomotive, *King George V*, now resides at STEAM, the Swindon GWR Museum.

Other stations facing the axe enjoyed short-lived reprieves. **Almeley Station**, for instance, closed in 1917 (during the First World War) only to re-open in 1922. It shut permanently in 1940 (during the Second World War).

Others survive only in miniature: such as at **Broomy Hill Railway**, outside Hereford town.

Current Services

There are now just three lines serving the county:

The **Shrewsbury & Hereford Railway** was the first to reach Herefordshire in 1853 (see p.132). Today part of the Welsh Marches line, it began as a joint venture between GWR and the London & North Western Railway (L&NWR).

Like the Hereford to Worcester (see below), it required an engineering solution to get through challenging terrain: notably the twin Dinmore Tunnels, opened in 1853 and 1891 respectively. Running beneath Queenswood Country Park and Arboretum, they held the last part of the track to be 'doubled', some thirty years (1893) after the rest of the route!

More important, perhaps, was the Hereford end – the earlier Barton Station, on the HH&BR, was unable to cope with up to four railway companies converging on the town, so Hereford Barr's Court was constructed – now the only survivor of the city's three sites (see above).

The **Newport, Abergavenny & Hereford Railway** (NA&HR) – latterly GWR – has been running services between Hereford and the south-west of Wales for more than 150 years. Intended to terminate at Hereford Barton, it first operated in 1853 and even now takes traffic into Hereford Barr's Court. Though many of the intermediate stations were lost under Beeching, Pontrilas Timber Yard bucked the trend. In 1997, it reopened a halt and extended the line in order to bring in essential supplies.

The **Hereford to Worcester** line linked the industrial furnaces of Birmingham and the Black Country with the rich coal seams of Wales. Opening a stretch from Worcester to Malvern came as early as 1859, but it took a further two years before the line burst through the dense Malvern Hills and on towards Hereford.

The entire project hung on its greatest achievement: Ballard's 1,567yd long Colwall Tunnel. From an initial progress of 10ft a week, things ground to a crawl, with just 6in a day, excavated by hand! Following a major collapse in 1907, missing a goods train by a wing and a prayer, a new tunnel was dug, opened in 1926 and used to this day. The old tunnel survived and was used to store military shells during the Second World War.

A third tunnel, at Ledbury, and the Leadon Valley viaduct – containing thirty-one arches and 5 million bricks – still carries the track as part of the modern Cotswold Line.

Footnote: **Colwall** is the only village in Herefordshire to retain a working station (unmanned).

ROADS

Long before today's overused roads, Herefordshire's fortunes were shaped by ancient trackways and the construction of new routes. From drovers' roads to motorways, the story of moving through the county is full of surprise.

Prehistory

Prehistoric trackways often hugged the scarps of the Herefordshire hills. One, stretching from Woolhope to Yatton, edged along Marcle and Ridge hills to Oldbury Camp. Another, the Ridgeway, continued for several miles, passing beneath the Herefordshire Beacon (British Camp) and arriving at Eastnor down to the south. An Iron Age **trackway** at Brandon Camp (Adforton) came out of the hillfort before it too headed south.

Roman

Few of the Roman's great arteries penetrated the county. Those that did owed more to quashing the Welsh and securing their natural resources.

Watling Street, the major Roman route from Wroxeter (*Viroconium*) to Caerleon (*Isca Silurum*) enters Herefordshire near Leintwardine (along the line of High Street) before bypassing Wigmore and Mortimer's Cross. It enters *Magna* (Kenchester) and the villa at Bishopstone, before crossing the Wye near The Weir, and on to the south. It soon becomes Stoney Street, running dead arrow-straight towards Madley and Kingstone. Skirting Abbey Dore and Longtown, and the Walterstone villa, it exits the county on its way to Abergavenny (*Gobannium*).

A separate road up from *Glevum* (Gloucester) takes in the industrial settlement of *Ariconium* near Weston-under-Penyard, before arcing south towards Monmouth (*Blestium)* and on into Usk (*Burrium*).

Another from *Ariconium* runs off northwards to Blackwardine (near Leominster). Passing Fiddler's Cross at the B4224, it skirts Fownhope, Mordiford, Bartestree and Withington, and finally Saffrons Cross before reaching its end.

Yet another, running east through Stretton Sugwas, was possibly part of Watling Street or a separate one altogether. It is still shown on the local OS maps as 'Roman road' which, as everyone knows, runs as straight as a die. Skirting modern Hereford and Holmer, it reaches Weston Beggard, Stretton Grandison and down towards Ashperton, before leaving the county at its border with Dymock.

Other possible roads – all veins rather than arteries – have yet to yield evidence as firm as these four.

(Sources inter alia: www.htt.herefordshire.gov.uk and Cooke n.d.)

Medieval

The medieval 'hollow ways' (or 'sunken roads') were once a commonplace feature, linking settlements, markets and points in between. The county has almost 500 examples: one extends between Little Birch church and the Axe and Cleaver Inn (a true road to ruin!?), while another runs from Bollitree Castle to Linton's Fiddler's Cross. One on high ground, on Altborough Hill, descends near Hoarwithy down to Wiggle Brook (near Tresseck). (Source: Hurley 2007: pp. 5–6).

Industrial

So-called 'lime kiln ways' (e.g. Hurley 1992) were routes to and from these industrial centres. Many have become public rights of way, and several can be found at Little Dewchurch, Sollers Hope, Fownhope, Woolhope and Whitchurch.

Droveways

According to Wayne Smith, in *The Drovers' Roads of the Middle Marches* (see bibliography), a network of routes allowed Welsh cattle to be driven to market. Moving slowly enough to limit exhaustion, but sufficiently quick to avoid sluggish decay, Smith reveals the clues to finding these early Herefordshire highways.

Place names reflect the burgeoning trade:

- Stanky or Biswal (referring to dung!)
- Halfpenny (the sum paid for overnight grazing)
- And places in London, reflecting the main destination for these Welsh knights of the road (e.g. Piccadilly, Little London)

Many of the routes, though, went to nearby markets, including Bromyard and Ledbury (and no doubt some more), while others hooked up with the highways to Oxford or similar cities having links to the east.

The main routes Smith has recorded include:

- From Builth Wells to Newchurch, arriving at Rhydspence (see also p.89) and on towards Hereford via Staunton-on-Wye (note here London Farm);
- Llandrindod via Stanner, the Fforest Inn (another renowned haunt of the drovers) and down into Kington;
- Newbridge-on-Wye, Glascwm and Gladestry, over Hergest Ridge before reaching the town;

- And a network of routes from Hay towards Hereford, exploiting the rugged Black Mountains as well as the valleys and commons alongside the Valley of Gold. (Source: Wayne Smith 2013)

Turnpikes

The turnpike roads were intended to improve England's roads and ensure its new burgeoning wealth. And by the time of the 1730 Act, Herefordshire already had the nation's largest network. Selected county turnpikes (with their modern designations) below:

- Hereford to Whitney (A438)
- Bromyard to Upper Sapey (B4203)
- Kington to Willersley (A4111)
- Hereford to Welsh Newton (A466)
- Ledbury to Ross (A449)
- Dorstone to Pandy (unclassified)

A tollgate at **Widemarsh**, outside what became the Essex Arms pub, controlled the turnpike road into the town. The inn has since been removed to Queenswood Country Park!

Milestones were the other major development, being a legal requirement since 1766. Some twenty-seven are listed in Herefordshire, including in Longtown, Welsh Newton, St Devereux and Clifford. (Source: NHLE)

Routes of the Living ... And Their Dead

Monastic Ways, Corpse Ways, Bier Ways – all evocative names for routes of the clerics or for the last ride of the dead. Monks' Walk from St Bartholomew church to Hellens, Much Marcle is long-associated with the eleventh-century French monks who founded the site, while a bier way runs from Hentland church to St David's burial place near Harewood End. (NB: wheeled biers are preserved in the churches of Hentland and Sellack.)

Modern Roads

Many ancient routes have become modern roads, but others – newer and larger – lace Herefordshire's lands:

M50 , from junction 8 of the M5 at Strensham, to Ross-on-Wye – this dual two-lane motorway has remained largely unaltered since it opened in 1962. As a strategic route into South Wales, it connects with ...

... the **A40**, one of Britain's oldest and most significant roadways, running from Fishguard to London. Re-routed between Abergavenny and Ross-on-Wye, creating the seemingly interminable stretch past Raglan before joining up with ...

... the **A449**, from Stafford to Newport, again via Ledbury and Ross.

Accidents and Tragedies

Between **Dinmore** and **Moreton-on-Lugg**, just after New Year's Day in 1861, the Shrewsbury to Hereford passenger train suffered a broken axle. All four carriages detached from the engine, careered down an embankment and landed upturned in a water-filled ditch. Two women were drowned in the second-class carriage. Astonishingly, within two and a half hours, the line had been cleared, the stricken engine removed and the passengers and their luggage conveyed to Hereford town.

On 12 February 1865, the boiler of the 1.25 a.m. goods train from Hereford exploded at **Leominster Station** whilst awaiting a signal. Being early, few people were caught up in the blast, the driver himself enjoying a lucky escape – vacating the cab only moments before. He wasn't alone. The force demolished a nearby goods shed, peppered the station house with impromptu ordnance but left its sleeping occupants unscathed in their beds.

The worst tragedy in living memory saw a passenger train from Manchester to Milford strike two cars on the level crossing at **Moreton-on-Lugg**. A road-vehicle passenger was tragically killed, her husband seriously injured. An investigation into the incident, which occurred on 16 January 2010, blamed the raising of the barriers *before* the train had passed through the crossing.

12

CRIME AND PUNISHMENT

As long as there are humans, there is crime. And as long as there is crime, there is punishment. What distinguishes one generation from the next is how it controls its lawless. Herefordshire has had its share of felons and villains – and its own means of restraint.

HEREFORDSHIRE GAOLS

Herefordshire County Gaol

Built 1792–97, the gaol stood on Bye Street Without (now Commercial Road). Designed by John Nash, who gave the nation Marble Arch and Brighton's Royal Pavilion, it is the only building from the time still standing today in Union Walk. The new Governor's House was built during alterations in the 1880s.

Its flat roof accommodated the gallows, where public hangings were held until 1868. However, the view from the street was obscured by a parapet wall, which was later removed and public disappointment appeased.

The gaol finally closed in 1915, after which it was only used to detain First World War deserters. Demolished in 1929, the site is now the Country Bus Station.

(Until the late eighteenth century, it was customary to appoint widows as Hereford gaolers.)

Hereford City Gaol

Opening in 1844, it closed just three decades later when its function was subsumed into the County Gaol. Standing on Grope Street*, since renamed Gaol Street, it has housed first the police station and then, until 2001, the magistrates' court. Both are now situated on nearby Bath Street. Currently (2015), the gaol is a church.

*Presumably sharing its origins with a street of that name in Bristol, another favourite haunt of the so-called 'four-penny knee tremblers'.

Hereford Bridewell

The Bridewell existed in the seventeenth century, housed in the old Water Gate to the west of Castle Green. It later became part of the new County Gaol.

Old County Gaol, St Peter's Square

Erected on the site of Shire Hall, this former county gaol held prisoners of all class (felons and debtors), in conditions that made John Howard (prison reformer) recoil in dismay. Attempts to get prisoners on the old straight and narrow must have been constantly tested, not least by the proximity of the Sign of the Fleece Inn. Now the Golden Fleece pub, its ale was passed through the windows to the prisoners below!

Other County Prisons

Thomas Lord Coningsby's failed attempt to open a new county gaol and assizes in **Priory House, Leominster** led to this thirteenth-century building becoming the 'lock-up' and workhouse.

Leintwardine 'Lock-Up': Its entrance, now bricked-in, remains visible at the junction of Church Street and High Street in the heart of the town.

Other prisons (see also Medieval Prisons, below) could be found at:

- Wilton, near Bridstow, to the north of the Wye
- New Street Prison, Leominster
- Old Gaol, Ross-on-Wye, now a private (more unusual) home

(Source: www.htt.herefordshire.gov.uk)

MURDER! MURDER!

Two of Herefordshire's historical murders include:

Don't Slay the Ferryman!
Before the days of the toll bridge at Whitney-on-Wye, a simple ferry took passengers across to Clifford and vice versa. At some point in history, the ferryman used to gather his takings in a pot he kept under the seat. With his last two passengers safely across, he made for home, unaware the two men followed behind.

The robbery was as violent as it was mean, and in the struggle the old boatman suffered a terrible blow. Whether they intended to kill him or not, the two murderers snatched up the coins and repaired to the inn.

The hostelry at Rhydspence, an old drovers' pub, was much favoured by locals. When the men paid with coins they took from the pot, the two were observed and quickly arrested. A search for the pot's rightful owner only yielded his corpse and the two bungling killers were tried and hanged at Hereford, on the site popularly known as Gallows Tump (near Belmont).

Stone the Crows!
In 1840s Longtown, a story of murder became overly touched by tales from the grave. A well-to-do shepherd, working out in the fields, had somehow incurred the wrath of two brothers, farmers, who seizing their chance, stabbed the poor man before stealing his purse. As the old boy lay dying, he was said to have uttered a hideous curse.

Calling down one of the crows from the nearby trees, he warned his would-be assassins that if they finished him off the crows would tell all. Laughing off the ridiculous caution, the two men completed their task and left for a life free of their foe.

Days later, the curse of the crows appeared to come true. Whenever the murderers entered the village, the birds gathered and circled and pecked at their eyes. For weeks they were assaulted until, remorseful and frightened, they were heard discussing the curse.

A search of their home found the victim's belongings and the pair were tried and hanged at Hereford Gaol. As they went to the gallows, the people recalled a gathering of crows … still known today as a 'murder' of crows.

MEDIEVAL PRISONS

The Bishop's Prison

It was the law, for a time, that every bishop in England should retain a prison for offenders of ecclesiastical (and, often, state) law. In 1547, the will of a Hereford citizen, concerned at conditions the felons endured, made a bequest:

> to the prison house within the palys, to remain to the prisoners there for them to lye upon, a flocke bedde, a bolster, a pair of blanketts, a coarse pair of sheets, and a coverlet (Johnson 1882).

'Byster's Gate' Prison

This formerly stood on the site of the present Kerry Arms Inn, at the junction of Commercial Road and Union Street. During the reign of Henry VIII, it remained possible – at least for those who could afford surety (bail) and were free men of the city – to be restrained within 'Bothe-halle' (Booth Hall) instead of the regular, more uncomfortable prison.

Forbury Prison, Leominster

It was said to have been housed in the West Gate of the priory in Church Street. Local courts occupied the upper floor. Owen Tudor was held here after the Battle of Mortimer's Cross, before being taken to Hereford and summarily killed.

MEDIEVAL JUSTICE

According to Johnson (1882), the following punishments were meted out in medieval Hereford:

- The gouge stool – made of wood and resembling the more familiar stocks
- The tumbrel, alternatively called the ducking stool or the cucking stool – a Saxon contraption in which the offender, often a 'cucking or scolding woman', was secured in the seat and plunged in the water (see the Leominster Ducking Stool, below)
- The pillory – again made of wood, took its name from the French *pilleur* (plunderer/pillager). Only men were once punished this way, facing ridicule and abuse from their neighbours and foes, but latterly both sexes were treated the same!

Whipping posts can still be seen at Eardisland and Fownhope, the latter joined by the old village stocks beyond the churchyard.

Mary, Elizabeth I and Henry VIII all enforced the Saxon custom of preventing travellers being boarded at inns for more than a day and a night. Intended to prevent the hiding of unsavoury characters, those found breaking the law would be expelled from the city and/or 'whipped at the cart tail' by the beadle (bedel).

An ancient Welsh punishment from *Archenfield* is worthy of note:

> There are some curious passages in Domesday relating to the customs which governed this little state within a state … If an Archenfield Welshman … slew another Welshman it was ordained that the relations of the slain 'meet together and plunder the slayer and his kinsmen and burn their houses until about noon on the morrow when the dead man's body may be buried.' Of this plunder the king took a third …
>
> (Bradley, 1906: 27)

The king then sequestered a third of the booty, while the rest remained with the avenging family.

THE LEOMINSTER DUCKING STOOL

A rare complete ducking stool is still housed in the town's priory church. Most often associated with punishing cuckolding women, it was frequently used in punishing men – in their case, in effluent water. '[B]utchers, bakers, apothecaries and brewers who cheated on measures or sold inferior food' were similarly punished (www.htt.herefordshire.gov.uk).

The name cucking stool was once believed to be a corruption of the word choking, while the Domesday book records it as *cathedra stercoris* (literally, chair of manure). Other French terms include *trebuchet* (or *triburch*) while the Latin *terbichetum* suggests the same derivation. Yet another offering is the French *coquine*, a sturdy beggar woman (or slattern) who was said to be cleansed (in body and mind) whilst strapped to the chair! However, the Saxon *scealping* is the one generally accepted.

> The Leominster machine was last used for a ducking in 1809 – the last known case in all England – when a Jenny Pipes refused to desist her abusive behaviour and was paraded around before being submerged in the Kenwater river. Eight years later, Sarah Leeke was likewise paraded, but the water was too low and she avoided the duck.

(Taken from the interpretation panel in Leominster church)

EXECUTIONS

The 'short-drop' gallows on the roof of Hereford Gaol were used until 1868. Executions in public were forbidden by law later that year. Afterwards, the new 'long-drop' scaffold was used, tucked away in the yard and having a trapdoor and pit.

The last hanging in the city was of William Haywood, a 61-year-old father of two. After bludgeoning his wife, he attempted to dispose of her body at Pokehouse Wood Quarry, Lucton, stupidly using a wheelbarrow to carry her corpse. Of course, he was seen and quickly arrested.

As an ex-inmate of a local asylum, his plea of temporary insanity was dismissed by the jury at the Shire Hall court. Instead, on 15 December 1903, he was transferred to the gallows at Hereford Gaol, where he was executed by national hangman, Henry Pierrepoint (father of Albert, his more infamous son). Two of Haywood's daughters were allowed to attend. According to custom, his body was not sent for anatomical dissection but interred in a grave under the yard.

The Hay Poisoner

Though the offices of Major Herbert Rowse Armstrong, a practising solicitor, were 'over the border' in Hay-on-Wye, his crimes were contrived at his Herefordshire home in nearby Cusop. Tried at Hereford Assizes in April 1922, he was charged with attempting to murder a rival in business – as well as the historical killing of his unfortunate wife.

Kitty Armstrong, four years his junior, had been ill for a considerable time. By August 1920 Hincks, the local doctor, was unable to fathom a cause, but her condition was now affecting her mind. Admitted to Barnwood, a private asylum on the outskirts of Gloucester, she remained as a patient for several months.

By the time Kitty came home, on 22 January 1921, both her physical and mental health had greatly improved. Yet, in a matter of days, the symptoms returned. On 22 February, she gave up the fight. According to Hincks, cause of death was gastritis, nephritis and a disease of the heart.

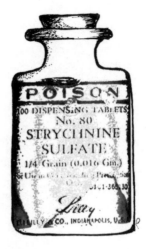

That would have been that, but for a careless act by the newly bereaved. Embroiled in a professional tussle over the sale of some land, Armstrong invited his adversary, Oswald Martin, round to tea. In true Agatha Christie style, he poisoned the man with one of the cakes.

It wasn't the first time. Martin and his wife now recalled receiving a surprise box of chocolates just weeks before, the consumption of which had left them both gravely ill.

Any suspicions, though, were all circumstantial until Davies, a pharmacist in nearby Hay – and father-in-law of the unfortunate man – recalled selling Armstrong packets of arsenic, supposedly for poisoning the weeds. So strong were the rumours, that not only was Armstrong arrested but poor Kitty's body was quickly exhumed. To no one's surprise, it was found to contain large traces of arsenic.

Armstrong was found guilty of poisoning Kitty and was hanged at Gloucester on 21 May 1922. He remains the only solicitor in Britain to be hanged for murder.

13

RELIGION

Herefordshire churches provide an unusual collection of facts, myths and legend. Whether architectural or spiritual, fact or fancy, much has been handed down through the generations. What follows is but a selection.

THE CATHEDRAL CHURCH OF ST MARY THE VIRGIN & ST ETHELBERT THE KING

Hereford Cathedral has experienced a rich and turbulent past. While many events are covered elsewhere in this book, the following are more notable moments in the sacred and secular life of the county's Episcopal seat:

Not Just the One ...
Today's majestic construction was not the first. Its origins, though, are uncertain. In AD 676, Putta (possibly not, as many believe, the Bishop of Rochester) established a see, either in Hereford, Ledbury or elsewhere west of the Severn. Nonetheless, there was a cathedral at Hereford (presumably in timber), to receive St Ethelbert's bones in 794 (see p.161).

Some time before 1055, Athelstan, Bishop of Hereford, rebuilt the cathedral (in timber or stone?). His own tragic demise came later that year when the Welsh ravaged the town.

The present Norman cathedral – the first built for certain in stone – was constructed on the orders of Reinhelm (c. 1107–15), probably not Robert de Losinga (c. 1079–95) (Pevsner 1963). It has since experienced multiple styles – 'original' Saxon, Early English, Geometric, Perpendicular and Gothic – from a number of famed architects, all for better or worse.

The central tower – erected at the height of Thomas Cantilupe's fame (see also p.160) – was adorned with ballflower decoration – as was the old west tower, before it collapsed in 1786 (see below). The 'repair' work by eighteenth-century architect, James Wyatt, did little to improve its failing regard. In fact, according to many, he only made matters worse! His rebuilt west end was a particular gripe, remodelling the nave, removing one of the bays and the entire Norman gallery. So unpopular was his work it was itself replaced by Oldrid Scott's incarnation, completed in the early twentieth century and the one still seen today.

Disaster and Death

On Easter Monday, April 1786, the old west tower suddenly collapsed, taking half of the nave and wrecking the aisles. Miraculously, no one was killed, but nearby buildings, including the Cathedral School, were evacuated to avoid further risk.

However, when a falling stone struck the scaffolding, later erected to undertake the repairs, several workmen fell with it, all to their deaths.

The wooden spire, rising 92ft above the central tower, was judiciously removed to lessen the load on the nave.

The old Chapter House was lost in 1769, having fallen into decay once the lead from its roof had been stripped during the siege of Hereford in 1645.

Too often, the cathedral has been the home of mischief and misrule: for instance, the choirboy, overlooked for the solo, who disrupted his rival's moment of glory by releasing a monkey which, of course, ran amok; or the organist and choirmaster, John Farrant, who in *c*. 1583 arrived from Salisbury Cathedral with a terrible past. Less than a year before, leaving midway through matins, he had attempted to murder the Cathedral Dean! Failing to appear at his subsequent hearing, he was later chastised ... for his vile and inappropriate conduct in Hereford choir!

(Source: Vaughan 2014)

Eye-catchers

The King's Chair – a rare thirteenth-century seat still seen in the choir. It has carried at least one monarch's rear, the self-styled King Stephen (see p.177).

Two shrines in the north transept, according to Pevsner (1963), are 'outstanding among any of their time in England':

- **St Thomas Cantilupe**, occupies the north transept and is the best preserved medieval shrine (base) in England – note the carved knights, probably Templar as Thomas himself was once the Provincial Grand Master.
- Nearby is **Bishop Peter Aquablanca** d. 1268. Traces of the original colours can be seen by more inquisitive eyes.

The shrine of **St Ethelbert the King** resides in the Lady Chapel, to the east end of the church (see p.161).

The **Hereford Screen**, by Sir George Gilbert Scott, was crafted in metal by Francis Skidmore of Coventry. It was shown at the International Exhibition of 1862 prior to its erection within the cathedral crossing. Fashioned in copper, iron and brass, and adorned with the carved flowers of passion, it contained some 300 cut polished stones. Dismantled in 1967, it is now housed in the V&A London museum who undertook their largest ever conservation programme, costing £800,000.

The **misericords** date from *c*. 1360. Pevsner regards them as some of the best. Multiple carvings include:

- fox and geese (see also Churches – Canon Pyon)
- stag and hound
- lion and lioness
- a mermaid
- a lute-playing goat (!)
- a cauldron
- woodwoses (mythical 'wild men')

The **Audley Chapel** is a rare two-storeyed chantry, *c*. 1500 (see also p.158). Nearby is the tomb of **John de Swinfield** (d. 1310), with sixteen swine carved around the arch (a pun on his name)!

Bishop Stanbury's Chapel is *c*. 1470s, fan-vaulted with later Arts and Crafts windows: a mermaid is seen carved in the stone.

A bagpiper and mermaid come together in the outlandish carvings inside the North Porch.

Claims To Fame
The crypt is Early English, dating to *c*. 1220 – the only other in England of a similar date underpins Rochester Cathedral.

A fireplace sits in the south transept wall – the only other in such a position is in Durham Cathedral.

One of the cathedral's original doors bears linen-fold carving – the earliest known in England.

From Dean to King's Chaplain
Cardinal Thomas Wolsey, perennial thorn to Henry VIII, was once prebend then dean of Hereford Cathedral, *c*. June 1509. Much later, he was Archbishop of York and as Henry's chaplain was instrumental in diplomatic relations at the Field of the Cloth of Gold. So popular was he that Henry repeatedly tried to have him made Pope. Yet with the row over divorce from Catherine of Aragon, and the king's subsequent break from the Catholic Church, Wolsey soon became Henry's irritant sore. Facing arrest on charges of treason, he died on 30 November 1530, aged 60 – a broken but resolute man.

And Finally …
Leofric, Mercian earl and his infamous wife, Lady Godiva, endowed the cathedral with large tracts of land (see also p.158).

While Hereford Cathedral was not to everyone's liking, William Cobbett, on his *Rural Rides* through the county, lamented its state in unequivocal terms:

> [Worcester Cathedral is] indeed, a poor thing, compared with any of the others, *except that of Hereford*!

CHURCHES OF HEREFORDSHIRE

A random selection of noteworthy things:

(I must highlight here the excellent *Harris's Guide to Churches and Cathedrals*, from which much of what follows was sourced (see bibliography). And to my dear friend, Ann Large, who selflessly gave it me as a much-treasured gift.)

The county boasts nine rare detached towers. St Mary, Pembridge is an absolute gem, of a type more usually found in the county of Essex (Pevsner 1963) – its interior forest of timber and pyramidal roof gives a Scandinavian feel. The massive thirteenth-century example at Holy Trinity, Bosbury formed part of the defences resisting the Welsh. Other examples were later attached to their church. Garway, Holmer, Ledbury, Canon Pyon, Kington, Richards Castle and Yarpole all finish the list.

Madley's Nativity of the Blessed Virgin Mary, described as 'one of the finest and most spacious village churches in England', remains largely unaltered since the thirteenth and fourteenth centuries. It boasts a newly restored and accessible crypt. Other features point to its eleventh-century origins, while six stained-glass roundels in the east window date from the thirteenth. A statue of Mary, believed to have once stood in the crypt, drew pilgrims to witness its ethereal powers, while others were called to this, the birthplace of St Dyfrig, credited with crowning Arthur, the mythical king.

St Bartholomew, Much Marcle has several green men, the pagan symbol of growth and rebirth – a nod to a pagan past. One here is considered unique – wearing a cross and chain draped around his neck: tangible proof of the Christian transition?

Kilpeck – a Norman 'Carved Church', Settlement and Castle
Approaching Kilpeck from a south-easterly direction, one is afforded a dazzling tableau of Herefordshire's past. Cheek-by-jowl lie three monuments of medieval life:

The **church of St Mary & St David** is a gem like few others. Built in 1135, and described as 'one of the most famous Norman churches in England' (Harris 2006), it occupies the raised, ovoid site of a small Saxon minster; in this case it replaced an earlier 'cell' of St Pedic (hence Kilpedic to Kilpeck).

Its intense Norman carving is original work without, it is claimed, substantial repair (those inside apparently have none). The exterior corbels attract the greatest attention: an elephant, crocodiles, juggler/tumbler, Equus Dei (it's usually the *Lamb* of God, not a horse!), green men, sheela na gig, dog and hare ... all topped by its *pièce de résistance*, the south door. Here, medieval warriors join an angel that's flying, a phoenix and Pisces the fish. Everything is crowned by the great Tree of Life – all carved by the Herefordshire School of Romanesque Sculpture (see p.103), it is an esoteric confection of Christian and pagan beliefs.

To the immediate west are the earthwork remains of Kilpeck Castle. Built in timber *c*. 1090, but soon after superseded in stone, its founder was William FitzNorman, given the *vill* by William the Conqueror. Only two (partial) walls now remain, but each has a hearth and the whole structure, on a sizeable motte, evokes past ages.

Completing the medieval triumvirate, north of the church and northeast of the castle, are earthwork remains. This once moated settlement evolved alongside its neighbours, until something or someone forced its people to leave.

More Churches

A lewd carving, quite out of place in **All Saints, Hereford**, shows a character exposing himself in obvious fashion! Almost certainly never meant to be seen, it was placed out of sight and left for future generations to find.

The church in **Clodock** is probably built on the site of its patronal saint's tomb – **St Clydog/Clydawg**. It hosts treasures which include a triple-deck pulpit, musicians gallery, medieval paintings and a nineteenth-century tomb.

Several Herefordshire churches host depictions of dragons, unsurprising given their neighbourly Welsh. At **Holy Rood, Mordiford,** the image (now gone) on the outside west wall was said to respect the Wales–England divide. A more modern design – of St George slaying the dragon – adorns the inside south wall of **St Michael's church, Breinton.**

St Michael's church, Garway, renowned for its round nave (not surviving), is believed to have been founded in the twelfth century by the noble Knights Templar, succeeded by the Knights Hospitaller, who placed the new chancel roof. It is said to be one of the finest in the county. The once-detached tower, built in *c*. 1200, was connected to the nave three centuries later. Elaborate carvings – in the Islamic style – tell of long-past crusades and secrets of old.

Herefordshire's churches are renowned for their fonts: **St David's, Much Dewchurch** claims to be Saxon; **St Mary's, Foy** has the biggest in the county; and – so many believe – **St Mary Magdalene,** Eardisley has the nation's finest Norman example.

In **St Michael, Michaelchurch,** a Roman inscription bears the following message: *EO TRI(VII) BECCICUS DONAVIT ARA(M)* – 'To the god of the three ways (crossroads), Beccicus dedicates this altar'.

St Catherines, Hoarwithy, known as the Italianate church, is the lavish product of nineteenth-century incumbent William Poole. Distressed by the 'ugliness' of his existing chapel, he had it 'converted' into a Romanesque-Byzantine anomaly in this rural corner of England. Painted columns, green-and-white marble pulpit and a peacock mosaic – all exemplify his desire for a more 'beautiful' form.

The Arts and Crafts church of **All Saints, Brockhampton** (near Ross) is another Herefordshire church of unusual type. Completed in 1902, as a private commission, its design – by architect William Lethaby of the Central School of Arts and Crafts – followed their established principles, employing local craftsmen and vernacular techniques. The result is a modern gem, based on the medieval plan but encapsulating William Morris' nineteenth-century passions. Perhaps its most endearing feature is its charming thatched roof, one of 100 (or less) in the whole of the country. It also possesses an embroidered altar cloth by Burne-Jones.

Misericords at **St Lawrence, Canon Pyon** carry several carvings, including a wheel of St Catherine and a fox with the geese. These and the Holy Rood (chancel screen) are both said to have come from a nearby friary, lost under the Dissolution and Henry VIII (note nearby Friar's Grove).

St Mary Magdalene, Leintwardine reveals its turbulent past, with walls 6ft thick to a height of 76ft. Troubles came not just from the Welsh – Romans conquered the people, the Saxon fought the Viking, and the Normans asserted their manorial 'rights'.

And finally ... Some Herefordshire churches enjoy isolation, replacements or originals now quite out of place. Divorced from their once-thriving settlements, Moreton Jefferies is a noted example. Often these villages were lost to the bubonic plague, though sometimes the cause was not quite so ghastly. Earthwork remains survive at Preston Wynne, Stockton Bury, Hampton Wafer and Edvin Ralph.

WOODEN YOU KNOW IT!

The oldest ecclesiastical effigy in wood can be found inside the border church of St Mary the Virgin at Clifford. Dated *c.* 1280, depicting an anonymous priest resplendent in robes, it bears traces of orange still seen in the folds. The example at St Bartholomew, Much Marcle, about eighty years younger, is nearly as rare, revering a layman, Walter de Helyon, of nearby Hellens. Another in Wolferlow church is believed to be the oldest in England portraying a woman.

The wooden font at King's Pyon is one of just thirty-two known to survive. Those at Aston Ingham (St John the Baptist) and Burghill (St Mary) are in lead, hardly less rare. At St Mary in Foy, the font has oddly ten faces, while St Mary in Marden has a total of twelve. Around Herefordshire, so-called chalice fonts are unique to the county.

Hereford Cathedral's Chained Library has the oldest depiction in brass of a king of these isles: St Ethelbert the Martyr, seen tucked in a rare thirteenth-century depiction of Thomas de Cantilupe.

DID YOU KNOW?

A palindromic plea for spiritual cleansing can be found on the font of St Peter & St Paul, Leominster: 'ΝΙΥΟΝΑΝΟΜΗΜΑΤΑΜΗΜΟΝΑΝΟΥΙΝ'. It reads the same backwards as forwards, and is Greek for 'Wash my sins and not my face only'.

A rare glass sundial from *c.* 1710 sits in the window of St Michael & All Angels, Ledbury.

The last medieval church crypt to be built in this country is at Madley's Nativity of the Blessed Virgin Mary.

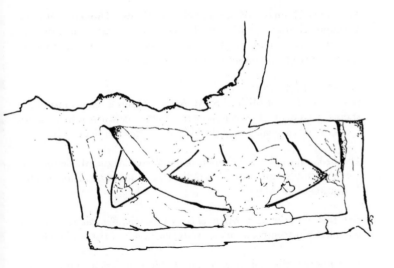

The twelfth-century St Mary the Virgin at Welsh Newton saw the last chantry chapel constructed in England, in 1547. The stone screen is a rare survivor from the pre-Reformation, while a fish etched on the thirteenth-century porch is a timeless reminder of the Christian ichthus design. The grave of St (Blessed) John Kemble draws hundreds of pilgrims (see p.162).

STAINED GLASS IN HEREFORDSHIRE

Pevsner (1963) regarded Herefordshire 'a most rewarding county' for its early stained glass. The following, both ancient and modern, is a small sample from the area's churches:

Iconic Characters

A window in St George's, Woolhope, is said to depict **Lady Godiva**, naked protestor and Earl Leofric's famed femme fatale, alongside her sister, Wulviva (as in Wulviva's Hope or Woolhope). It commemorates their generous bequest of three manors to Hereford Cathedral. 20th century.

The saints Thomas à Becket and Hereford's own Thomas Cantilupe are captured together in Credenhill church. The rare depictions are apparently so accurate that they must have been made pre-Reformation (though it remains a mystery how they survived).

Ancient and Modern

In the church of **St Michael & All Angels, Mansell Lacy**, most of the stained glass in the chancel is modern. But the east window in the south aisle contains a small glazed shield from the fourteenth century.

The medieval windows at **Nativity of the Blessed Virgin, Madley** include six thirteenth-century roundels in the east window, one depicting the Adoration of the Magi.

The east window of **St Michael & All Angels, Kingsland** is a near-complete fourteenth-century treasure, including Christ in His Glory.

In **Hereford Cathedral** are what must be Hereford's newest treasures in stained glass. The four **Traherne Windows** (Audley Chapel) are vibrant and modern, commemorating the seventeenth-century cleric and poet Thomas Traherne who, many maintain, was secretly ordained bishop at the end of the Interregnum (see p.107). Designed by artist Tom Denny, alumnus of the esteemed Edinburgh College of Art, his other works include the new Richard III window in Leicester Cathedral.

A **Millennium Window**, crafted for St Michael in Brimfield, shows the Dove of Peace ascending on high.

Stained Reputations

St Mary, Eardisland has a fine east window from 1901, by the Birmingham company, Burlison and Grylls. Significantly contains a shard of medieval glass.

All Saints, Hereford has work by two leading lights: designers Clayton & Bell, and the Arts and Crafts stalwart, Margaret Aldrich Rope.

Thomas William (T.W.) Camm's window at **St Andrew, Hampton Bishop,** is widely considered one of his best.

From Macbeth to Morgan

View Shakespeare's plays recorded in stained glass at St Michael the Archangel, Felton, installed in commemoration of former vicar and thespian, the Revd John Henry Evelegh. An enthusiast of the Bard, he put on his plays for no doubt grateful parishioners.

The classic British-made Morgan motor, although developed in Malvern, is said to have had its origins in nearby Stoke Lacy – as a three-wheeler prototype built in the rectory garage of St Peter & St Paul! Two stained-glass windows depict the Morgan connection: a pair of early three-wheelers, one red, one blue, are joined by a 'regular' Morgan, their factory and P.H.G. Morgan, the founder's son and respected church patron.

A Timeline of Majesty

All Michael & All Angels, Eaton Bishop hosts 'the finest decorated glass in the country … ', according to Pevsner (1963). He refers to the glorious east window dated *c.* 1320–40.

A rare favourite in glass, the **Jesse Tree** depicts the Virgin Mary (and thus Christ) descended from Jesse, father of David, King of the Jews. A fine partial example exists at the **Nativity of the Blessed Virgin, Madley,** with a splendid early twentieth-century version at **St Peter's, Bromyard.**

In the south aisle of the nave of **Hereford Cathedral,** a stained glass depicts King Charles I triumphantly entering the city after quelling the Scots.

CULT OF THE SAINTS

In medieval Europe, a religious fashion emerged in response to the perceived power of the saints. Relics and reliquaries (caskets) became the focus of prayer, and of those who saw profit in pilgrims ... We start at the cathedral.

St Thomas Cantilupe
The chief saint of Herefordshire is St Thomas de Cantilupe. His shrine was said to have witnessed more than 400 miracles – second only to Thomas à Becket.

As Bishop of Hereford 1275–82, he was 'a man of exceptional character; selfless, discerning, courageous and deeply spiritual' (Alington 2001): consecrating Dore Abbey before yielding to a personal scandal and a powerful foe.

In 1282, John Pecham, Archbishop of Canterbury and once Thomas' tutor, excommunicated the bishop from the Catholic Church. His reasons were probably linked to diocesan rights.

The now distraught former bishop travelled to Rome, and pleaded his case with Pope Martin IV. He at least gained Absolution – for his part in the spat – but before a full conclusion was reached, Thomas died from a fever.

As was then custom, the bones and the heart were removed from his corpse and sent back to England. His other mortal remains were buried at San Severo monastery (Alington 2001: p. 147), overlooking Orvieto. The bones were interred beneath a slab in the old Lady Chapel of Hereford Cathedral, the site quickly becoming 'the most visited [shrine] in western England' (Alington 2001). So many came that their offerings alone paid for the new (current) central tower.

In April 1287, his remains were translated to a new shrine in the north transept, presumably to accommodate his continuing fame. Miracles were reported on Easter Monday, and soon the public demanded he be honoured a saint.

This presented a problem, for Pecham at least. To be canonised while excommunicated was not just sacrilegious, it was frankly impossible. However, in 1320, some thirty-eight years after his death, the outspoken demands of King Edward II made the improbable real. Claiming Cantilupe *was* reconciled to the Church via the Pope's Absolution, John XXII pronounced Thomas a saint. His feast day was set as 2 October.

Now all St Thomas needed was a new, permanent shrine; better equipped for a saint such as he. It was installed in the old Lady Chapel, and his remains translated there in 1349 ... Though this was not an end to his troubles. In *c.* 1538, with Cromwell's erosion of all Popish ways, his shrine was completely destroyed, but not until his relics were squirrelled away.

And that would have been that, but for one final twist. The abbey at Belmont, south-west of the city, was apparently presented with a fragment of bone – claimed to be part of St Thomas's skull. Indeed, his relict remains were said to have been carried through Hereford to ward off the plague in 1610.

The shrine today – including the original thirteenth-century base – has been magnificently adorned. Still in the north transept, it attracts a new wave of visitors – pilgrims and tourists alike.

St Ethelbert
A well in Marden churchyard marks the head of a spring, said to have burst forth where King Ethelbert died.

Slain in AD 794, on the orders of a conniving (or coerced) Mercian King Offa, Ethelbert, the 14-year-old East Anglian leader had been invited to marry Alfreda, Offa's daughter, at nearby Sutton Walls.

For reasons unknown, he won not a heart but instead lost his head. And whether for gain or base human duplicity (some say for land, others for spite), the sorry loser in love met a premature end.

Wracked with a sense of remorse, Offa had the body taken to Hereford Cathedral, where he re-dedicated the church to St Mary the Virgin and St Ethelbert the King.

At Ethelbert's tomb, miracles were soon being witnessed. A cult of St Ethelbert became an inevitable fact. Indeed, such was its draw for the sick and the pious that his tomb was still being visited until the 1300s at least. (Some say Bishop Athelstan's eleventh-century cathedral was paid for by the offerings of pilgrims.)

Meanwhile, in Quay Street to the south-east of the cathedral, a twentieth-century fountain recalls a second holy well, said to exist in what is now St Ethelbert's House. Its medicinal properties were firmly believed well into the 1900s. When it was cleaned, in the century before, its base was found to be coated in pins – tokens of hope to this benevolent saint.

Other 'Herefordshire' Saints

St Clydog/Clydawg, after whom the village of Clodock is named, is believed to have been buried where the oxen pulling his funeral bier stopped by the River Monnow and refused to go on. He was once King of Ewias, martyred *c.* AD 500.

Following a vision, **'Saint' Katherine (Audley) of Ledbury** (though never actually canonised) established a hermitage within the sound of the church bells that rang without playing. The place of her enlightenment is still known today as 'Saint' Kattern's Stone. (Not to be confused with St Katherine of Antioch, after whom the hospital (almshouses), chapel and Master's House are all named (see pp. 30 & 105).

St (Blessed) John Kemble, a Catholic martyr during the 'Popish Plot', fell foul of Captain Scudamore of Kentchurch in 1679. He was hung, drawn and quartered on Widemarsh Common, but only after finishing a meal and enjoying a smoke (forever more known as 'smoking a Kemble pipe'). Beatified in 1929, his left hand is enshrined in St Francis Xavier's church, Broad Street in Hereford.

FRIARIES AND PRIORIES

Due to its border location, Herefordshire had plenty more castles than houses of God. Nevertheless, many were founded in the nine centuries between Christianisation and Henry VIII's new Anglican Church. As always, the following is not exhaustive.

At the time of Henry VIII's Dissolution, there were twenty-one monastic centres in the county, as listed below in 1804. Tanner's *Notitia Monastica* (1744) was slightly at odds: replacing Shobdon and Dewlas with Acley (Lyre Ocle) and Hamm (Holme Lacy) – with additional entries for 'lesser houses' at Bromyard and Dinmore.

Aconbury	Ewyas	Lymebrook
Barton	Flanesford	Monkland
Clifford	Hereford (4)	Shobdon
Crasswall *(sic)*	Kilpec *(sic)*	Titley
Dewlas	Ledbury	Wigmore
Dore	Leominster	Wormsley

(Source: Duncumb 1804)

Leominster

In Llanllieni (later Leominster), an early religious centre was inspired, according to legend, by a chance meeting between a holy man and Merewahl, the Mercian royal (who undoubtedly founded the house in *c.* AD 660). In separate dreams, the former fed a lion from his hand and the latter, Merewahl – also known as The Lion – received news from a holy man on the future site of his church. On the spot where they met, Merewahl constructed a minster – traditionally described as a house of nuns, though modern thought now favours both sexes.

Nonetheless, in AD 770, the Welsh ravaged Leominster and slew all its nuns. The town's current name honours Leofric, Earl of Mercia, who restored the old nunnery before 1066 (Leon's Minster).

In *c.* 1046, the boisterous Sweyn, son of Earl Godwin and brother of (later) King Harold, abducted the Abbess Edgiva (Godiva?) and made her his own. As a result, the nunnery was dissolved. In a case of religious and misogynist bias, her tale was recounted in 1808 by the Reverend Rees:

164 *The Little Book of Herefordshire*

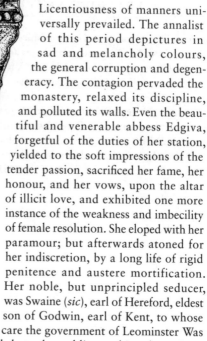

Licentiousness of manners universally prevailed. The annalist of this period depictures in sad and melancholy colours, the general corruption and degeneracy. The contagion pervaded the monastery, relaxed its discipline, and polluted its walls. Even the beautiful and venerable abbess Edgiva, forgetful of the duties of her station, yielded to the soft impressions of the tender passion, sacrificed her fame, her honour, and her vows, upon the altar of illicit love, and exhibited one more instance of the weakness and imbecility of female resolution. She eloped with her paramour; but afterwards atoned for her indiscretion, by a long life of rigid penitence and austere mortification. Her noble, but unprincipled seducer, was Swaine (*sic*), earl of Hereford, eldest son of Godwin, earl of Kent, to whose care the government of Leominster Was particularly intrusted, but who, adding to his other crimes treason and rebellion against his sovereign, King Edward the Confessor, and experiencing many reverses of fortune, died a miserable exile in a foreign land: demonstrating by the example of his fate, the necessity and importance of subjecting passion to the control of reason and religion, and resisting the first and early seducements of vice.

(With thanks to Joyce Marston of Stockton Bury)

Today's church (what remains) owes its beginnings to a new priory built *c.* 1120–3, by the Abbots of Reading. Over the years, two further naves were added and the monks and their livings spread out from the town. The relict fishponds at nearby Kimbolton could be a splendid example.

Hereford Clerics

The **Franciscan grey friars** (from the colour of their robes) – friary founded in the early 1200s by Sir William Pembrugge, on a site now recalled in the name of a bridge. One of its burials was Owen Tudor, the 'never-was' king killed by the future Edward IV after Mortimer's Cross (see p.72).

The **black friars of St Dominica** – from 1322, occupied lands in Widemarsh (*Wigmarch*), which Leland described as the 'fayrest Suburbe of the Towne'. Situated behind Coningsby Hospital (see p.105), there survive rare upstanding remains including the only complete example of a cemetery preaching cross of this Mendicant Order.

St Guthlac's Benedictine priory – once in the area beneath Castle Green, excavations have found plausible evidence for an old burial ground. The house was translated *c.* 1143 to a site near the modern Commercial Road. Believed to have moved under the auspices of Bishop Robert de Bethune (*c.* 1131–48).

The hospital of St Giles – stood beyond St Owen's Gate, toward the Ledbury Road.

Out and About

One of the more notable abbeys in the west of the country, at **Dore**, was founded in 1147 by Robert Fitz Harold of Ewyas, grandson of William I. With extensive possessions given by generous kings, Robert Lord Ewyas undertook the construction of a glorious edifice, home to the order of Cistercian monks. However, with crippling costs, additional money was raised only when Peter Aquablanca, Bishop of Hereford, promised twenty-one days excuse from doing penance for those contributing to the cost of the work! At the time of the Dissolution, Dore Abbey was said to be worth in excess of £100 per annum. And such was their standing that Edward I – he of the castles of Wales – entrusted Dore's abbot to secure the oath of allegiance from the stricken Prince of all Wales (Llywelyn ap Gruffydd).

From the thirteenth century, an Augustinian nunnery stood on a spot in **Aconbury Forest**, right up to Henry VIII's Dissolution. Founded by Margery (Margaret) de Lacy, Lady of Trim and wife of Walter, Lord Meath, the land of 'three carucates' was assigned by King John, just over a week before his death on 18 October 1216. The present church of St John the Baptist is likely the sole intact remains of that priory's estates.

Titley Priory, a rare cell of Tiron in France, was established as a branch of the order of Benedict, founded *c.* 1220/21, and dissolved in 1391.

The **Grandmontine Priory** at Craswall was one of that rarer French order. During the Hundred Years War, its French monks were watched for signs of collusion, and Edward III insisted their revenues be sequestered to keep them from enemy hands. He need not have worried: the friars were starving and had little to share.

The priory lands at **Lymbrooke** (*Lymebrook*, *Lindbroke*) near Eardisland were later appropriated for Williams' Hospital, and included a farm known as Nunsland.

The Augustinian priory at Wormsley, of the order of St Victor, was founded by Gilbert Talbot in the reign of King John. It was dedicated to St Leonard de Pionia.

The refectory of **Flanesford Priory**, Goodrich, established 1346, is now a hotel, though evidence of its cloister has been found at the rear. It was a small Augustinian house of canons regular, founded by Sir Richard (Second Lord) Talbot of Gotheridge (Goodrich) Castle.

Wigmore Abbey, the largest in Herefordshire, had an itinerant start. Founded at Shobdon before 1131, it moved to Eye, then to Wigmore, on to Beodune (Byton?) and back whence it came. In 1179, the monks settled in their house north of Wigmore, an Augustinian abbey in which eight of the Mortimers were subsequently buried and whose walls were ravaged by the dissolute king!

Clifford Priory was established in the time of Henry I (r. 1100–35), to the order of Cluniac, or Benedictine reform. Founded by Simon FitzWalter (according to Leland), or the fantastically titled Simon FitzRichard-FitzPonce (*Notitia Monastica*).

14

HERITAGE II

GREAT FAMILY ESTATES

A county so rich in history is obliged to have its fair share of country estates. From Marcher Lords to Roundheads, entrepreneurs to Royalists, many great families (and landholders) made Herefordshire their home.

Great Estates of Herefordshire
Here is a handful 'open' to the public (at the time of writing):

Berrington Hall – so vast, it covers three parishes! At the centre sits one of Henry Holland's earliest masterpieces of English architecture. Built in the late eighteenth century, its parkland was the work of Capability Brown, while the outbuildings include a former laundry, restored tiled dairy and a purpose-built coachman's home-cum-shooting lodge.

Brockhampton Estate – still a working farm, this 1,800-acre estate has its roots deep in Herefordshire's past. The medieval manor, set on an island in the midst of the estate, stands out as the jewel in the crown. Complete with moat and timber-framed gatehouse, it is obligatory when here to step back in time. It is an absolute gem. The nineteenth-century parkland includes literally miles of walks.

Holme Lacy House – later seventeenth century, Grade I listed manor house, probably built for the 2nd Viscount Scudamore and his bride, Frances Cecil. Almost certainly contains elements of an earlier house on the site, which itself was by no means the first! All set in what was once a medieval deer park. The house has an orangery, while the estate includes fishponds, steward's house, stables and kennels. It was home to Britain's first school of equitation, *c.* 1600. The whole building is now a hotel.

Downton Castle – situated at the delightfully named Downton on the Rock, this eighteenth-century pile commands both its landscape and architectural history. Its founder, Richard Payne Knight, was instrumental in the Picturesque movement, blending different periods into a singular house. The registered parkland and gardens span a gorge hosting the River Teme, large parts of which form the National Nature Reserve (see p.46).

Historic Family Seats

- Harley – Brampton Bryan Castle and Berrington Hall, Leominster
- Scudamore – Holme Lacy and Kentchurch
- Roger de Lacy – Weobley and *Ewias Lacy* (Longtown)
- William de Braose – Huntington Castle, Kington
- Ralf de Mortimer – acquired Wigmore Castle after its FitzOsbern founders were evicted for dissent against William I. Mortimer's son brought a similar fate, backing the future King Stephen against Henry I's preferred successor, the Empress Maud (Matilda)

Major Landholders in Domesday

In days when possession was nine tenths of the law, the largest holders of land, after the king and the Church, were recorded as follows:

Nigel the Physician	Robert Gernon
Ralph de Todeni	William son of Norman
Ralph de Mortemer	William son of Baderon
Roger de Laci	William de Scohies
Roger de Mucelgros	Henry de Ferieres

Great Landholders of the Nineteenth Century

The largest (private) landholders at the start of the period were:

Duke of Norfolk	Earl of Essex
(through marriage to the	Sir George Cornwall
Scudamores of Holme Lacy)	Mr R.P. Knight
Earl of Oxford	Mr Somerset Davies

Holders of lesser estates included:

Mr Charles Bodenham of Rotherwas   Mr J. Kedward of Westhide
Mr T.A. Knight of Elton   Mr J. Apperly of Withington
Mr J. Phillips of Bringwyn

BRIDGES

For a county defined by its rivers, it is perhaps no surprise that bridges are essential to Herefordshire life. Of some 178 in the county, at least fifteen are recorded as medieval. Eight are scheduled and a further seven listed Grade I or II*. Here are a few of the more celebrated ...

Wye Bridge, Hereford

Famed six-arch, fifteenth-century bridge with v-shaped 'cutwaters' (for both function and refuge). This Grade I listed and scheduled treasure (see NHLE) links St Martin's with Bridge Street and the city beyond.

The earliest bridge was constructed in timber, stone not being used until *c.* 1100.

Two charters of Richard II (1383) made provision for the repair of the bridge, much damaged by a great Hereford flood. Timber and stone were granted from the royal De la Haye Forest, which once came up

close to the gates of the town. Levies on trade and other activities were charged if the money was used for maintaining the bridge, and the following tariff was set:

> For every two thousand onions for sale, one farthing. For every ten sheaves of garlic for sale, one farthing. For every small cart or wain of sea fish, one halfpenny. For every horseload of sea fish, one farthing. (Johnson, 1882: 55)

At the time of Elizabeth I (r. 1558–1603), butchers and meat factors had to deposit their waste alongside the bridge:

> that all offal and refuse from the slaughter-houses should be carried away in the night and taken to Wye Bridge, there to be cast in at the place accustomed, between eight and nine o'clock in winter, and nine and ten in summer. (*Ibid*: 127)

One of the arches was rebuilt after the siege of Hereford in 1645. Another forms part of the cellar of a house on the south.

More recently, the bridge has been used in a TV commercial – promoting a particular cider!

Mordiford Bridge, Mordiford
This splendid sixteenth-century bridge (with fourteenth-century features) is one of Herefordshire's oldest examples. It crosses the Lugg near the site of a ford. Evidence of an even earlier version has been deduced from inspecting the fabric, and its unusual profile at the far eastern end. Although the river typically flows through just two of its (unusual) nine arches, all have taken the water during times of flood. The bridge is said to have meant much to composer, Edward Elgar (see p.109), with the view from the bridge believed to have inspired his 'Elegy for Strings (Op 58)'.

Lugg Bridge, Lugwardine
Aptly named bridge over the river, dating from fourteenth century with later additions and repairs using original material. Links Lugwardine with Stapleton. Repairs to this triple-arched gem were recorded in a medieval text (the fifteenth-century Episcopal registers of Hereford). In an evocative discovery, a Saxon spearhead was recovered from the river below the bridge, dropped or lost perhaps while crossing the much earlier ford.

Wilton Bridge, Ross-on-Wye
A Grade I listed, late sixteenth-century bridge, with great cutwaters and resulting angled refuges at parapet level. Six curved arches span the Wye, linking the parishes of Bridstow and Ross-on-Wye. It is the main route into town, running south-east from the bridge before turning north-east and up to the centre. An ornate, four-sided sundial holds its position in one of the parapet refuges, casting an eye to the ways of the past. The faded inscription once read:

> Esteem they precious time – Which pass so swift away –
> Prepare thee for eternity – And do not make delay.

Described in its listing as '[a]n exceptionally fine stone bridge' (NHLE).

Bredwardine Bridge, Bredwardine
The bridge was built in 1762–64, and restored 1921: its brick fabric is enhanced by stone dressing. Six-arched with triangular cutwaters, it links Brobury with Bredwardine overlooking a 'beach'. Made famous in the writings of the local vicar and diarist, Francis Kilvert (see p.63), who recorded numerous, often tragic events: a coach and its horses spilled into the river, their heads held under by the bearing reins, so that one (a wheeler) perished beneath the coach, and the other (a leader), having pulled itself clear, 'plunged and pawed and reared at the bridge' before being swept away by the current (Plomer 1944: p. 89).

Dry Arch Bridge, Goodrich
A scheduled monument, this early nineteenth-century bridge, south-west of Priory Farm, spans the busy B4229. One of the earliest flyovers to carry a minor route over a major road, without the need for an inconvenient junction. (Or, as the county previously recorded: 'an excellent example of very early vehicle grade separation'(see NHLE).) It has one arch and includes some thirty-three steps, linking pedestrian traffic between the two roads.

Forge Bridge, Downton on the Rock
One bridge effectively divided in two on the Downton Castle estate. The first part, a so-called accommodation bridge (maintaining historic rights of access), spans the Teme. The second portion, extending a short distance to the south, crosses an old race. The first and larger arch is twice as great as the other, while the entire is some 80yd long. Built *c.* 1772, possibly by the surveyor Thomas Farnolls Pritchard, designer of the Iron Bridge at Coalbrookdale. The bridge is met by the Herefordshire Trail (see p.87) and has a nearby weir.

Footbridges

Suspension Footbridge, Sellack

Elaborate footbridge linking Sellack with King's Caple. Built in the late nineteenth century, the maker's plate declares 'Louis Harper A.M.I.C.E. Maker Aberdeen'. Constructed as a suspended walkway over the Wye, it is enhanced with columns and finials, made all the more attractive by its location.

Victoria Suspension Footbridge, Hereford

Built in *c.* 1897/98 to celebrate Queen Victoria's Diamond Jubilee. Latticework towers join with terracotta piers and Victorian lamps. It affords a fabulous view of the town and cathedral. It was erected with the help of public subscription and can be accessed via Castle Green on the one side, and Mill Street/Wye Way on the other. It has replaced an earlier ferry near the site.

Toll Bridge

Whitney Toll Bridge still operates at the princely sum of £1 per vehicle (at time of writing), linking the parishes of Clifford and Whitney-on-Wye. Built 1802 (with some subsequent alterations), the roadbed is timber with iron gratings atop five sturdy stone arches, the southern-most one now askew. Grade II listed and one of just eight privately owned toll bridges in the UK still exempt from taxation (after an Act of Parliament in 1796).

MILESTONES

Though originally a Roman invention, most milestones today herald the age of the turnpikes (see Transport – Roads). They began life as flat plates or signs (frequently made of timber, then stone and finally iron), but were subsequently 'angled' for easier reading, as the new speedier coaches flew by. More than twenty in the county are listed.

Milestone Treasure Hunt (just for fun – observe yours and others' safety and the Highway Code!):

A 40, Weston-under-Penyard
A 4137, Hentland
A 4137, Marstow (three)
A 438, Clifford
A 465, Allensmore
A 465, Haywood
A 465, St Devereux
A 466, Llangarron

A 466, St Weonards (two)
A 466, Welsh Newton
A 49, Much Birch
B 4228, Walford (two)
B 4347, Bacton
B 4348, Dorstone (two)
B 4348, Peterchurch (two)

And one for mile*posts* (apologies for any duplication):

A 466, Llanrothal
A 466, Llanwarne
A 466, St Weonards
B 4352, Madley

B 4521, Garway
B 4521, Hentland (two)
B 4521, St Weonards (two)

(Source: NHLE)

DOVECOTES

Very much a Herefordshire 'industry', the county retains a wealth of these old 'towers of delicacy' (i.e. from eating the *squabs*). Scattered amongst historic estates, gardens and farms, they were typically round and constructed in stone. Many though were fashioned in timber, which – this being Herefordshire – were beautifully painted in black and white squares. They include the oldest known relict (fourteenth century), though the practice was apparently imported with William I.

Garway (not open to the public) – built 1326 (possibly reusing an earlier version), the oldest known dovecote to survive in Britain: 'AD 1326 this pigeon house was made by Brother Richard.'

Stockton Bury Gardens (open to the public) – possibly medieval with eighteenth-century repairs; includes its original revolving ladder, used when collecting the squabs from the 500+ nest holes – a large number suggesting monastic origins.

Credenhill – octagonal, brick and smaller in form. Built about 1800, it remains in private hands, but is said to be visible from a nearby lane.

Luntley – seventeenth-century treasure of black-and-white timber, square-built with wooden framing inside. A later addition – the brick 'kennel' – housed a terrier or perhaps a cat as a deterrent to rats. Appears slightly skewed!

Staunton Park (gardens open by appointment) – rare hexagonal *pigeon* house, brick-bonded, with approximately 300 nest holes.

Gaines, Whitbourne – a rare form, thought to date from the late seventeenth century. Square-built, red brick, to a height of 6m, hides both a dovecote of 500 nest holes and a circular icehouse below. The latter extends beneath ground about 2m. Door to icehouse at ground level; that to dovecote is 2m above. Private.

15

ROYALTY
AND POLITICS

Herefordshire's place at the heart of England's constitutional history is too often ignored. Yet so often it played a critical role, witnessing more than its fair share of political intrigue and royal conspiracy...

ROYAL PATRONAGE

Pre-Conquest monarchs who made Herefordshire 'home' include: Offa (at Sutton Walls, Marden), Athelstan (who secured loyalty from the Welsh when he met them at Hereford), Alfred the Great and Edward the Elder (responsible for first fortifying the town), the ill-fated Harold II (Godwinson) who, before losing the nation, re-strengthened the town in 1062; Stephen, Maud, even King John, Queen Isabella, Richard III, Charles I and II – and no doubt many others besides.

A RANDOM SCATTERING OF LOCAL EVENTS ...

Edward the Confessor came to Hereford's rescue in 1062, ending years of invasion by the troublesome Welsh. Through Harold II (see above), he eradicated the danger by destroying its prince (see Chapter 4).

In *c*. 1120, Henry I added the lands of Leominster to his abbey at Reading, leading to the former's new priory.

King John, who signed Magna Carta, frequently made Hereford Castle his home. When under assault from Louis of France, he made the city his headquarters for a week in July 1216.

In *c*. 1231, Henry III resided at Hereford as he attempted to quell the troubles with Wales.

In the early 1400s, King Henry IV – the first Lancastrian king – headquartered himself in the city, better placed for administering attacks on Glyndŵr's Welsh. He had previously married Mary de Bohun, a descendent of one of the most powerful families in the post-Conquest county.

ANARCHY AND SACRILEGE

During the twelfth-century wars of The Anarchy, Stephen and Matilda (Maud) left more than their mark on the county's inhabitants – both dead and alive …

In late spring 1138, Stephen took the castle at Hereford where, for several weeks, he established his court. According to some, he repaired to the cathedral and 'crowned' himself king – though, perhaps with more accuracy, he is said to have attended Mass on Whitsunday, celebrating his victory by wearing the crown and sitting in what has become the famous King's Chair (see Hereford Cathedral).

After taking Weobley Castle from Geoffrey Talbot (see p.59), Stephen left Hereford Castle in the hands of his men, only to learn the following year of its loss to the supporters of Maud. As her local in chief, it was during Talbot's siege that the greatest atrocities were wreaked on the cathedral. Dead bodies, many only just buried, were pulled to the surface as his fighters excavated the graveyard to embattle the ground. Great warring machines then desecrated the tower, from where they laid siege on the castle beyond. (An irate Stephen turned back toward Hereford, but only reached Little Hereford near Leominster before beating retreat.)

In 1143, Stephen faced temporary confinement in old Wilton Castle, until Martel his steward sprang his escape.

THE 'SHE WOLF' OF HEREFORD?

Rebellious Isabella, estranged queen of Edward II (r. 1307–27), established her court at Hereford Castle after slighting the king (see below).

On her hit list of enemies was Hugh Despenser the Younger, who she saw hanged from a 50ft-high gallows. His final demise, on 24 November 1326, was especially unkind. For it was not enough that he die, but that his name and reputation should be extinguished forever.

The debacle leading up to his death began as he was marched into town. Clothed in a vestment, his arms were reversed. And on the rear were written the first six verses of Psalm 52, including: 'Why boastest thou thyself, thou tyrant ... ' A crown of nettles was then thrust on his head, as he was drawn on a hurdle to his gallows and hanged. But that wasn't the end. Still barely alive, he was cut down, disembowelled and beheaded – his suffering complete.

Another foe of the so-called She Wolf of France – Simon de Reding – met a similar end, though his nearby gallows were shortened by 10ft.

ROYAL FAVOURITES

Mortimers of Wigmore
An entire book could be written about the Mortimer line, but in a few short paragraphs there is room for just two:

Roger Mortimer, 1st Earl of March, took Queen Isabella as lover and liege, though his brutal intention was for only one thing: the throne of the nation.

On 23 September 1326, the pair sailed from France with the young Prince Edward – Isabella's son and heir to the throne – as their valuable cargo. Reaching England and Wigmore, they usurped the queen's husband (Edward II), and notionally placed the boy on the throne ... Only Edward III, being so young, required a regent, and the devious plan was almost complete. Both would govern the country as one.

A victorious Isabella had Edward II brought to nearby Ledbury – a captive – before she sent him to Berkeley and his unspeakable end. Instructing the gaolers to leave not a mark on the body, the men tried starvation with little success. The answer was rectal impaling – his bowels horrifically scorched on the end of a spit, no outer mark left should anyone ask. Whether lost in translation, it was supposedly done at Roger's command.

The pair could now rule without sanction, at least until Edward III's coming of age. But when the boy turned a man, he exacted revenge. Roger Mortimer was hanged at Tyburn on 29 November 1330.

Edmund Mortimer, 5th Earl of March, was 'a rudderless noble whose lineage placed him at the mercy of others' (*ODNB*). Though his line of descent from Edward III was 'weakened' by the female line, he was a political pawn whose death would lead to the Wars of the Roses.

Under Henry IV, he was feared as a rival, expected to mimic what went before (that is, his family's ambition). But Edmund had no desire for kingship, instead supporting the ascent of Henry V. Whilst fighting Henry's wars in Normandy he died from the plague in 1425.

No matter how reticent he had been about ruling his country, the missed opportunity indirectly provoked future struggles between Lancaster and York.

Blanche Parry of Bacton

Though not a royal herself, Blanche Parry of Bacton owed much to her favour at court, especially with Queen Elizabeth I. Her place in history also resides in her lifelong connection with St Faith's, Bacton parish church, where one of the oldest known depictions of the sixteenth-century queen still survives.

She was born in 1508, and christened at St Faith's. Parry's family owned nearby Newcourt and engineered positions of power through an illustrious connection to court life: Parry's aunt, Lady Troy, served as guardian to Edward VI and Elizabeth I, both children of course of Henry VIII. Her father, Henry Myles, was Sheriff of Hereford, and her cousin, Sir William Cecil, would become Elizabeth's Secretary of State.

Blanche's own royal connection started years earlier, rocking Princess Elizabeth's cradle in 1533. By the time she was crowned Queen of England twenty-six years later, Blanche had stayed in the court for nearly as long. Parry revealed herself a great scholar, diplomat and political fox. She took charge of the queen's library, brokered peace between the queen and Lord Leicester, and secured favourable returns for her neighbours in Herefordshire whenever she could.

But, above all, she remained Elizabeth's friend. As tensions erupted around the Catholic Queen Mary, she stuck by her side and advised on her plight. Forever Elizabeth's favourite, the queen granted her carriages, estates and copious wealth ...

Parry died on 12 February 1590, aged 82, one seldom loved more by a reigning monarch. Elizabeth ordered she be buried a baroness, a lofty title that reflected the queen's greatest affection. Her tomb, at St Margaret's church, Westminster, carries the inscription: 'Chief Gentlewoman of Queen Elizabeth's most honourable Privy Chamber and Keeper of Her Majesty's Jewels, whom she faithfully served from Her Highness' "birth".'

And her Herefordshire legacy? In the oldest known depiction of Elizabeth I – as an icon ('Gloriana') – Parry accompanies her in the monument on display in St Faith's: the two women, both unmarried, memorialised together – inseparable in death as they had once been in life. Blanche Parry's epitaph reads: 'With maiden Queen a maid did end my life.'

A Few Others

Robert Devereux, 2nd Earl of Essex, was for a long time Queen Elizabeth's favourite. Indeed, they were related (first cousin twice removed). Born in Netherwood near Bromyard in 1565, he was a consummate politician and eminent soldier. However, following his disasters in Ireland, and facing allegations of treason, his fall from grace led to his cruel execution in 1601. He was the last person beheaded at the Tower of London.

Sir Rowland Lenthall, Yeoman of the Robes to King Henry IV, built the forerunner of Hampton Court Castle in 1427, supposedly on the auspices of the reigning monarch.

Scudamore of Holme Lacy was granted the demesne of *Sancta Keyna* (later Kentchurch) for his part in bringing William the Conqueror onto the throne.

OF CHURCH AND STATE

At least four Herefordshire churches display royal armorial panels (coats of arms): one at **St Mary the Virgin, Monnington-on-Wye,** celebrates Charles II; another, in **St James the Less, Wigmore,** William IV – 'Silly Billy' who reigned 1830–37. Others are at **St Clydog's, Clodock** (to King George I); and one at **St Bartholomew, Ashperton** – of particular note for displaying the Plantagenet monarchs in reverse order, which was apparently a swipe at their part in the Wars of the Roses.

A HISTORY OF CONSTITUENCY

Herefordshire's role in national politics began early. From 1295, and possibly sooner, King Edward I sought representatives from the three boroughs of Hereford, Leominster and Weobley. Burgesses were sent in 1298. In 1304, Bromyard, Ledbury and Ross joined the ranks.

Pre-Civil War
From before 1628, the county and city of Hereford, Leominster and Weobley each sent two Members of Parliament, giving a total of eight. They did so until the Reform Bill of 1832.

The Long Parliament called by Charles I (1640) saw political opponents trading more than just words. Herefordshire men from each constituent borough fought one another on the field of war:

- Herefordshire County – Sir Robert Harley of Brampton Bryan (Parliamentarian) and FitzWilliam Coningsby of Hampton Court Castle (Royalist)
- Hereford City – Richard Weaver (died before all-out war) and Richard Seaborne (Royalist)
- Leominster – Walter Kyrle (Parliamentarian) and Sampson Eure (impartial)

- Weobley – Thomas Tomkins and Arthur Jones Lord Ranelagh (both Royalists)

Post-Civil War
Divided by monarch (between the Restoration and the reign of Queen Anne), a list of MPs returned by the county included:

Charles II (r. 1660–85)
Edward Harley & William Hinson, alias Powell
John Scudamore & Anthony Price
John Viscount Scudamore & Edward Harley, K.B.

James II (r. 1685–88)
John Morgan, Bart. & John Hoskyns, Knt. and Bart.
John Morgan, Bart. & Edward Harley, K.B.

William and Mary (r. 1689–1702)
John Morgan, Bart. (died)/Edward Harley, Knt. & Herbert Croft, Bart.
Herbert Croft, Bart. & Edward Harley, Bart.
Henry Cornewall & Henry Gorges
John Williams, Knt. & Henry Gorges

Anne (r. 1702–07)
John Williams, Knt. & Henry Gorges
James Viscount Scudamore & Henry Gorges
James Viscount Scudamore & John Pryce
James Viscount Scudamore & John Pryce/Thomas Morgan, Bart.
James Viscount Scudamore & Thomas Morgan, Bart.

Before 1832, the county was predominantly Tory, the Whigs scoring rare successes in 1774 (under Sir George Cornwell of Moccas Court), and in 1831 on the eve of reform. Since 1832, Weobley ceased to return any Members, though the county as a whole was awarded a seat, giving a revised total of seven.

The Redistribution Bill, passed in 1867, saw Herefordshire's seats reduced to six (one of Leominster's was lost). In 1885, the number was reduced again, to just three: Herefordshire North (Leominster), Herefordshire South and Hereford City.

'WELL DONE HEREFORD!'

The *Western Mail*, in 1893, saluted a 'glorious victory' for the pro-Unionist movement:

Well done Hereford! The most important election fought out for a great number of years past has resulted in a glorious victory for the cause of the Union.

Hereford is not a large constituency, but it is a typical English one. It is not too much to say that it elected Mr. W.H. Grenfell at the general election a great deal less because of his politics than from admiration of him as an athlete and of his robust, manly English character. It was Unionist before Mr. Grenfell's election, it is now Unionist again.

The defeat of the Gladstonian candidate at Hereford yesterday will have momentous results. The real meaning of Home Rule is understood now as it has never been understood before, bad as the Goverment Home Rule Bill is, it has, at any rate, had the effect of opening the eyes of the electors to the dangers, the perils, the injustices, to which it will open the door. Seeing and knowing and feeling all this, Hereford has cast its vote against the Government. The slight Gladstonian majority is now still more attenuated. The House of Lords will be strenghtened and encouraged in their determination to throw out the Bill as soon as it reaches them. The next general election is brought over so much nearer by the result of the contest yesterday.

Mr. E. Radcliffe Cooke desrves well all the hearty congratulations which have poured upon him. He has made the highest Conservative poll on record in Hereford, and has come out the encounter with a majority of forty-four where his Liberal predecessor had a majority of one hundred and twenty-seven.

MODERN REPRESENTATION

The county today returns just two Members of Parliament. In the General Election of 2015, the following votes were cast (winners in **bold**):

North Herefordshire
William David ('Bill') **Wiggin**, Conservative Party – 26,716
Daisy Blench, Green Party – 3,341
Jeanie Hay Helen Falconer, Liberal Democrats – 5,768
Jonathan Paul Oakton, United Kingdom Independence Party – 6,720
Sally Prentice, Labour Party – 5,478

Hereford and South Herefordshire
Alexander Jesse ('Jesse') **Norman**, Conservative Party Candidate – 24,844
Anna-Maria Coda-Hancorn, Labour Party – 6,042
Nigel Ely, United Kingdom Independence Party – 7,954
Lucy Ann Hurds, Liberal Democrats – 5,002
Diana Stella Toynbee, Green Party – 3,415

(Source: Herefordshire Council)

Since 1979, there have also been Members of the European Parliament, or MEPs (currently seven). In 2014, as part of the West Midlands Constituency, votes for the five top-scoring candidature parties in Herefordshire (using a form of proportional representation) were as follows (West Midland totals in brackets):

Conservative Party – 15,717 (330,470)
United Kingdom Independence Party – 15,450 (428,010)
Labour Party – 4,995 (363,033)
Green Party – 4,367 (71,464)
Liberal Democrats – 4,094 (75,648)

(Source: Herefordshire Council)

BIBLIOGRAPHY

OFFLINE

Alington, G. 2001, *St Thomas of Hereford*, Leominster: Gracewing

Alington, G. 1996, *The Hereford Mappa Mundi*, Leominster: Gracewing

Anthony, E. 1903, *Herefordshire Cricket*, Hereford: Anthony Brothers Ltd

Bannister, Rev. A.T. 1916, *The Place Names of Herefordshire*, self-published

Barratt, H.C. 1928, *Pear's Cyclopaedia* (33rd Edition), London: A&F Pears

Boden, A. 1992, *Three Choirs: A History of the Festival*, Stroud: Alan Sutton Publishing

Bradley, A.G. 1906, *In the March and Borderland of Wales*, London: Archibald Constable & Co.

Carless, W.T. 1914, *A Short History of Hereford School*, Hereford: Wilson and Phillips

Cobbett, W. 1830, *Rural Rides*, London: Thomas Nelson & Sons

Cooke, G.A.N.D., *Topographical and Statistical Description of the County of Hereford*, London: Sherwood, Jones & Co.

Coplestone-Crow, B. 2009, *Herefordshire Place-names*, Almeley: Logaston Press

Davies, Melanie, 2012, *Walk around Leaflet: Hereford Cathedral*, Hereford: Hereford Cathedral

Davison, C. 1899, *The Hereford Earthquake of December 17, 1896*, Birmingham: Cornish Brothers

Denning, A. & P. Ranger (eds) 1993, *Theatre in the Cotswolds*, London: The Society of Theatre Research

Dickens, C. 1867, *All the Year Round* (18), London: Chapman and Hall

Duncumb, J. 1804, *Collections Towards the History and Antiquities of the County of Hereford* (Vol. 1), Hereford: E.G. Wright

Eisel, J. & R. Shoesmith 2009, *Herefordshire Pubs*, Stroud: The History Press

Fenn, R.W.D. & J.B. Sinclair 2000, *The Herefordshire Bowmeeting. A Social History*, Kington: The Hergest Trust

Filmer, R. 1976, *Hops and Hop Picking*, Aylesbury: Shire Publications

Harding, M. 1998, *A Little Book of the Green Man*, London: Aurum Press

Harris, B.L. 2006, *Harris's Guide to Churches & Cathedrals*, London: Ebury Publishing

Havergal, F.T. 1887, *Herefordshire Words and Phrases. Colloquial & Archaic*, Walsall: W. Henry Robinson

Havergal, F.T. & H.G. Bull 1884, *Ancient Glass in the Church of St Mary, Credenhill*, Hereford: Jakeman & Carver

Hull, L.E. & S. Whitehorne 2008, *Great Castles of Britain and Ireland*, London: New Holland Publishers

Hurley, H. 2013, *Herefordshire's River Trade*, Almeley: Logaston Press

Hurley, H. 1992, *The Old Roads of South Herefordshire. Trackway to Turnpike*, Ross-on-Wye: Fineleaf Editions

Jakeman & Carver 1890, *Jakeman and Carver's Directory and Gazetteer of Herefordshire*, Hereford: Jakeman & Carver

Johnson, R. 1882, *The Ancient Customs of the City of Hereford*, London: T. Richards

Knight, T.A. 1811, *Pomona Herefordiensis*, Hereford: The Agricultural Society of Herefordshire

Leather, E.M. 2001 (1912), *The Folklore & Witchcraft of Herefordshire*, Penzance: Oakleaf Books

Lewis, G.C. 1839, *A Glossary of Provincial Words used In Herefordshire, And Some Of The Adjoining Counties*, London: John Murray

Lias, A. 1991, *Place Names of the Welsh Borderlands*, Ludlow: Palmers Press

Lord Ruthen 1816, *Miscellanea Antiqua Anglicana*, London: Robert Triphook

Matthews R. 2008, *Haunted Herefordshire*, Almeley: Logaston Press

Moir, A.L. 1964, *The Bishops of Hereford, their Cathedral and Palace*, Hereford: Jakemans Ltd

Mountney, Revd M. 1976, *The Saints of Herefordshire*, Hereford: Express Logic

National Trust 2015, *National Trust Handbook*, Swindon: National Trust

Oppitz, L. 2002, *Lost Railways of Herefordshire and Worcestershire*, Newbury: Countryside Books

Page, William (ed.) 1908, *Victoria County History Herefordshire*, London: Archibald Constable & Co.

Palmer, R. 2002, *Herefordshire Folklore*, Almeley: Logaston Press

Pevsner, N. 1963, *The Buildings of England. Herefordshire*, Harmondsworth: Penguin Books

Phelps, D. 2013, *Bloody British History: Hereford*, Stroud: The History Press

Phillott, Revd H.W. 1852, *The Days of the Flood Being the Substance of Two Sermons, Preached in the Parish Church of Staunton-on-Wye, Herefordshire on the Occasion of the Late Inundation*, Hereford: J. Head

Plomer, W. (ed.) 1944, *Kilvert's Diary 1870–1879. Selections from the Diary of the Rev. Francis Kilvert*, London: Jonathan Cape

Reade, Revd C. 1904, *Memorials of Old Herefordshire*, London: Bemrose & Sons

Rees, W.J. 1806, *The Hereford Guide*, London: Longman, Hurst, Rees & Orme

Robertson, H., Marshall, D., Slingsby, E. & G. Newman 2012, *Economic, Biodiversity, Resource Protection and Social Values of Orchards: A Study of Six Orchards by the Herefordshire Orchards Community Evaluation Project*, Natural England Commissioned Reports, Number 090

Robinson, C.J. 1869, *A History of the Castles of Herefordshire and their Lords*, London: Longman & Co.

Smith, W. 2013, *The Drovers' Roads of the Middle Marches*, Almeley: Logaston Press

Stanbury, D. 1993, *The Lady who Fought the Vikings*, Devon: Imogen Books

Tanner, Rt Revd Dr T. 1744, *Notitia Monastica*, Lowestoft: John Tanner A.M.

The Readers Digest Association (Ed.) 1980, *AA Book of British Villages*, London: Drive Publications

Treasure, R.N.D., *A Guide to Stockton Bury Gardens* (self-published)

Vaughan, D.J. 2014, *Bloody British History: Salisbury*, Stroud: The History Press

Walker, R. 2010, *The Dovecotes and Pigeon Houses of Herefordshire*, Almeley: Logaston Press

Whitehead, C. 1893, *Hop Cultivation*, London: John Murray

Williams, Revd J. 1808, *The Leominster Guide*, London: Longman, Hurst, Rees & Orme

Wright, J.P. 1819, *A Walk through Hereford*, Hereford: Watkins & Wright

ONLINE

Neither the author nor The History Press are responsible for the content of websites provided in this book (last accessed throughout 2015):

www.archiveswales.org.uk

www.bosci.net

www.breconbeacons.org/black-mountains

www.criminalunacy.blogspot.co.uk

www.forestry.gov.uk

www.herefordorchards.co.uk

www.herefordshire.gov.uk

www.herefordshire.gov.uk/leisure-and-culture/libraries/the-masters-house-project

www.herefordshirehistory.org.uk

www.historicengland.org.uk/listing/the-list (NHLE)

www.htt.herefordshire.gov.uk (including Herefordshire HER)

www.ledburymastershouse.blogspot.co.uk

www.loc.gov/pictures (Library of Congress)

www.magnacarta800th.com

www.malvernhillsaonb.org.uk

www.milestone-society.co.uk

www.oxforddnb.com

www.oxforddnb.com/view/article/37634

www.theguardian.com/books/2008/jan/19/fiction6

www.thekilvertsociety.org.uk

www.thelaskettgardens.co.uk

www.themappamundi.co.uk

www.victoriacountyhistory.ac.uk (VCH)

www.visitherefordshire.co.uk

www.visitherefordshirechurches.co.uk

www.woolhopeclub.org.uk

www.wyevalleyaonb.org.uk

ABOUT THE AUTHOR

DAVID J. VAUGHAN is a published author, historian, blogger, book reviewer, media presenter and public speaker. Former Assistant County Archaeologist for Wiltshire, since returning to Herefordshire's *Golden Valley* he has written and presented on different strands of the past. Often inspired by the brooding gaze of the 'unrivalled' Black Mountains, his family's links with the county stretch back more than 200 years. His previous titles include *Bloody British History: Salisbury* for The History Press.

Also from The History Press

GREAT WAR BRITAIN

Great War Britain is a unique new local series to mark the centenary of the Great War. In partnership with archives and museums across Great Britain, the series provides an evocative portrayal of life during this 'war to end all wars'. In a scrapbook style, and beautifully illustrated, it includes features such as personal memoirs, letters home, diary extracts, newspaper reports, photographs, postcards and other local First World War ephemera.